LISP

LISP

Christian Queinnec

Translated from the original French by
Tracy Ann Lewis
North Staffordshire Polytechnic Computer Centre

A HALSTED PRESS BOOK

JOHN WILEY & SONS
NEW YORK

© Éditions EYROLLES, Paris 1983

Authorised English language edition of
Language d'un autre type: LISP
first published 1983 by Éditions EYROLLES,
61 boulevard Saint-Germain, 75005 Paris

© English language edition, Macmillan
Publishers Ltd 1984

First published 1984 by
MACMILLAN PUBLISHERS LTD
Houndmills, Basingstoke, Hampshire RG21 2XS
and London

Published in the U.S.A. by
Halsted Press, a Division of
John Wiley & Sons, Inc., New York
Printed in Great Britain

Library of Congress Cataloging in Publication Data
Queinnec, Christian.
LISP / Christian Queinnec.
Translation of: Langage d'un autre type: LISP.
   Bibliography: p.
   Includes index.
   1. LISP (Computer program language) I. Title.
QA76.73.L23Q4513 1985   001.64'24 85-8635
ISBN 0-470-20226-2

   001.64'24   QA76.73'L23

Contents

Preface

LISP was conceived around 1960. At that time there were few high level languages in existence and even these were in their infancy. FORTRAN II was beginning to spread, ALGOL 60 was in the process of being defined and BASIC did not exist. Since that time, considerable improvements have transformed these languages, whereas LISP has remained virtually unchanged, a significant compliment to its creator John McCarthy. Historically, LISP has been linked with the development of Artificial Intelligence for which it has been the major programming language. The greatly increased interest in Artificial Intelligence in recent years has seen LISP established among the major languages. The last decade has witnessed the appearance of an ever-growing quantity of both theoretical and practical work concerning LISP.

LISP exists on almost all computers from the largest mainframe to the simplest micro, and there are even machines that have been specially designed for the language. Twenty years after its conception, LISP remains one of the better programming languages in existence.

This book intends answering three questions:

What is LISP?
How do we program in LISP?
What can we do in LISP?

It was not my intention to make the book simply a user manual (having to be linked to some sort of interpreter and therefore having to devote itself to dealing with the particular features of one system), or just a collection of commented examples (which risks focusing the reader's interest on the algorithms themselves rather than on the language in which they are written), or even merely a discussion of the language (describing its syntax and the semantics of its basic primitives but never touching the area of programming in LISP, its general techniques). If I seem to have ignored some areas of the subject, I freely admit that some concessions have been made to achieve the objectives set out above. A basic LISP nucleus is presented, which forms a solid foundation on which to build the rest of the LISP structure: one advantage of LISP is that it can, to a large extent, be defined in itself, and hence can possess such a simple 'core'. On this basis, four distinct programming styles are shown one after another, each explaining how LISP may be used efficiently. At the end of the book, programs describing a small software robot are given, which will familiarise the reader with the rudiments of what has become known as Artificial Intelligence.

I hope that this book will intrigue you, arouse your interest and finally win you over to LISP.

CHRISTIAN QUEINNEC

PART ONE
FIRST STEPS IN LISP

1 LISP Data

1.1 Atoms and Lists

The LISP nucleus comprises the *atom* and the *list*.
■ An atom is represented by a chain of contiguous characters, such as

ONE
ROSE
C6H5OH

or even

ACETYL-SALICYLIC-ACID

The atom represents a basic and indivisible piece of information (hence its name). Groups of information or more elaborate information are conveyed in the form of lists.
■ A list is a LISP object comprising

an opening bracket
object(s) separated by one or several spaces
a closing bracket

For example

(C6H5OH)
(1   PLUS 2 = 3)

The objects that may be contained in a list are called terms and are either atoms or lists. For example

((ACID (H2SO4 HCL))   (BASE (NAOH)))
 (3(FIRST ODD NUMBER (NOT PERFECT))
   (ENGLISH (T H R E E))
   (PLUS   1 2))

or even

((A ROSE) (IS (A ROSE)) (IS (A ROSE)))

This last list contains three terms, of which the first is a list (A ROSE) and the second and third are also each a list (IS (A ROSE)).
■ ( ) is known as the empty list. The empty list does not contain any object and therefore does not contain itself. (()) is a non-empty list whose single term is the empty list.

To summarise, any LISP object is either an atom or a list. Lists enable information to be represented in as complex or as structured a form as is required. The index of this book is a list where each term is a list representing a chapter, each chapter in the book is a list . . ., etc.

1.2 Primitive Handling Functions

Several functions are necessary in order to be able to handle these objects (lists or atoms): *First, Rest, Insert, Atom, Null* and *Eq.* These functions facilitate the building and decomposition of lists and can also be used to ascertain the nature of the handled objects.

In order to correctly define the scope and effects of these functions, we will use the following conventions.

As any LISP object (for historical reasons, we also use the term a Sexpression, short for 'Symbolic Expression', or to be more brief, an expression) is either an atom or a list, we can write the general statement

$$SEXP = LIST \cup ATOM$$

where

> LIST is the collection of lists
> ATOM is the collection of atoms

and where SEXP will therefore be the collection of LISP expressions.

Still speaking in general terms, $LIST - \{()\}$ will be the collection of lists apart from the empty list, in other words the collection of non-empty lists.

1.2.1 Definition of *First*

$$First: LIST - \{()\} \rightarrow SEXP$$

When applied to a non-empty list, the value of the function *First* is the first term of this list. Hence

> *First* applied to (C6H5OH) will yield the value C6H5OH
> applied to (1 PLUS 2 = 3) will yield the value 1
> applied to ((ACID (H2SO4 HCL)) (BASE NAOH)))
> will yield the value (ACID (H2SO4 HCL))

First is not defined for any other argument apart from a non-empty list.

1.2.2 Definition of *Rest*

$$Rest = LIST - \{()\} \rightarrow LIST$$

The function *Rest* complements the function *First*. When applied to a non-empty list, it takes this list as its value, with the first term omitted. Hence

Rest   applied to (A ROSE) will yield the value (ROSE)
      applied to (ROSE) will yield the value ()
      applied to ((ACID(H2SO4 HCL)) (BASE (NAOH)))
        will yield the value ((BASE (NAOH)))

Rest is not defined for any other argument apart from a non-empty list.

■ When suitably combined, these two functions allow the decomposition of any list. in other words, they allow any component to be accessed. For example. in order to obtain the first term of the third term of a list, we simply need to apply, in order, the functions *Rest, Rest, First, First* to this list; that is, the function

    First ○ First ○ Rest ○ Rest

which, when applied to ((A ROSE) (IS (A ROSE)) (IS (A ROSE))) will take the atom IS as its value.

1.2.3   Definition of *Insert*

    Insert: SEXP × LIST → LIST

Insert represents everything that is needed in order to make new lists. The function *Insert* builds a new list from arguments, the first of which may be anything, the second must be a list. The first term of the new list will be the first argument of *Insert* and the others will be those present in the list of the second argument. Hence

Insert   applied to A and (ROSE) will yield the value (A ROSE)
      applied to C6H5OH and () will yield the value (C6H5OH)
      applied to (A ROSE) and ((IS(A ROSE))) will yield the
        value ((A ROSE) (IS(A ROSE)))

■ You will notice that the functions *First ○ Insert* and *Rest ○ Insert* represent the first and second projections of SEXP × LISP on to SEXP and LIST respectively. In other words, when applied to a non-empty list, *First* and *Rest* enable you to find the actual arguments used when calling the function *Insert* to build this same list.

■ As a result of restrictions that limit the application of *First* and *Rest* to non-empty lists only, it is necessary to question the type of objects that are handled. This is possible by using the predicates *Null* and *Atom*. A predicate is a function whose result is a member of the set $\{tt, ff\}$ which represent the logical values True or False.

1.2.4   Definition of *Atom*

    Atom = SEXP → $\{tt, ff\}$

The value of the predicate *Atom* is True (that is, tt) if, and only if, its argument is an atom, otherwise its value is False (that is, ff). Thus

Atom   applied to (C6H5OH) will yield the value ff
applied to C6H5OH will yield the value tt
applied to (() C6H5OH) will yield the value ff

Atom may be applied to any object whatsoever.

1.2.5   Definition of *Null*

$$Null = SEXP \rightarrow \{tt, ff\}$$

The value of the predicate *Null* is True (that is, tt) if, and only if, its argument
is an empty list, otherwise its value is False (that is, ff). Thus

Null   applied to (C6H5OH) will yield the value ff
applied to C6H5OH will yield the value ff
applied to ( ) will yield the value tt
applied to (( ) C6H5OH) will yield the value ff

Null may be applied to any object whatsover.
■ The following predicate tests equality between two atoms.

1.2.6   Definition of *Eq*

$$Eq = ATOM \times ATOM \rightarrow \{tt, ff\}$$

The value of the predicate *Eq* is true (that is, tt) if, and only if, its two arguments represent the same atom, otherwise its value is False (that is, ff). Thus

Eq   applied to C6H5OH and ( ) will yield the value ff
applied to ( ) and C6H5OH will yield the value ff
applied to (A) and (A ROSE) will yield the value ff
applied to ACID and BASE will yield the value ff
applied to ACID and ACID will yield the value tt

Eq can give a result other than ff only when dealing with atoms.
■ What we have just described can suitably be called a data structure. Through-
out this book these will be defined according to the same format: objects and
operations.

The objects are divided into two classes: primitive objects (in this case, atoms
and the empty list) and compound objects (in this case, non-empty lists).

The operators are usually classed as:

(1) constructors (*Insert*) which make compound objects
(2) selectors (*First, Rest*) which decompose compound objects
(3) predicates or recognisers (*Null, Atom, Eq*) which determine the type or value
of objects.

We will meet similar approaches later on when we need to define adequate data
structures for certain specific problems.

1.3 The LISP Language

The LISP language is based upon three conventions, each of which will be discussed with comments.

1.3.1 Program and data identification

Convention 1: LISP programs are represented by lists.

As a program is simply a collection of information conveying how to carry out certain data processing, it may be expressed in the form of a list. By convention, we will denote

f(x), that is to say f applied to x, by the list (f x)
g(x, y) by the list (g x y)
g(x, h (y)) by the list (g x (h y))
f(g (x, h(y))) by the list (f(g x (h y))) etc.

Lists that represent programs are often called 'forms'. In the last example we have the forms

(f(g x (h y)))
(g x (h y))

and

(h y)

This notation is referred to as '(forward) Polish': The indication of the function precedes that of its arguments. The notation 'reverse Polish' consists in placing the function after the arguments to which it is applied, and is mainly used for pocket calculators.

In LISP

instead of writing x + y, we write (+ x y)
instead of writing 3x + 1, we write (+ (∗ 3 x)1)
instead of writing sin $\left(3x + \dfrac{\pi}{3}\right)$, we write (SIN (+ (∗ 3 x) (/ PI 3)))

In these examples we see that the atom + represents normal addition, and the atom SIN represents the sine function in trigonometry. The convention therefore requires that a name be given to the functions defined previously, in order that they may be used. It is quite suitable to call

First by the atom FIRST
Rest by the atom REST
etc.

We can write the following programs (the meaning of the 'quote' will be given in section 1.3.2)

(FIRST '(A ROSE)) whose value will be the atom A
(FIRST(REST '(A ROSE))) whose value will be the atom ROSE
(INSERT 'C6H5OH '()) whose value will be (C6H5OH)
(INSERT(FIRST '(C6H5OH)) (REST '(C6H5OH))) whose value will
        be (C6H5OH)

1.3.2 Logic values

Convention 2: The logic values tt and ff are represented by the two atoms:
T and NIL.

This convention enables predicates to be considered as functions whose resulting
values are members of the set $\{T. NIL\}$ and are included in ATOM, which is
itself included in SEXP. Therefore we may now write the following programs
(still ignoring the 'quotes')

(ATOM 'A) which gives the value T
(EQ 'A 'ATOM) which gives the value NIL
(ATOM(EQ 'T 'NIL)) which gives the value T, since whatever the
      outcome of EQ†, the result will be a logic value (tt or ff, in this
      case ff), and therefore an atom (T or NIL, in this case NIL).

■ If any program may be represented as a list, then inversely, any list is liable
to be considered as a program! In fact, if we wished to determine the first
term of the list

(INSERT 'A '(ROSE))

and if we write

(FIRST(INSERT 'A '(ROSE)))

we would obtain the atom A and not the atom INSERT as was intended.
    LISP provides a simple method to avoid this confusion. Strictly speaking, it
is not a convention; we will consider the technique in further detail later on.

    Any object preceded by a 'quote' must be considered as an expression and
not as a program.

Therefore, going back to the example above, we will write

(FIRST '(INSERT 'A '(ROSE)))

and this time we will get the atom INSERT.
    The following example shows the building of a program: the value of

(INSERT 'ATOM(INSERT 'T '()))

---

†Strictly speaking, *eq* is a function, and not EQ, which is an atom. But as the user does
not usually modify the natural link between EQ and *eq*, we will refer to the function
EQ (the function ATOM, etc.) and will abandon the notations *eq* (*atom*, etc.).

is the list

   (ATOM T)

which is a program whose value is the atom T.

■ By virtue of convention 1, programs are lists; lists disallow the presence of this 'quote', although it is nevertheless a very usual and practical facility. We should point out that

   '*expression*

is a typographical variant of

   (QUOTE *expression*)

Expression represents any LISP object. Hence, the program (QUOTE(C6H5OH)) returns the list (C6H5OH) as its value and may also be written as '(C6H5OH).

   The value of the program (QUOTE(ATOM 'A)) is (ATOM 'A) or (ATOM(QUOTE A)) according to whether you wish to write everything or condense the format of this resulting list. The value of the program (QUOTE QUOTE) is the atom QUOTE, which in no circumstances should be written as a single 'quote', since our convention stipulates that the 'quote' always precedes an expression and is not used on its own.

   This typographical convention is necessary because of the very frequent use of this construction.

1.3.3   The empty list

For historical reasons derived from the very first implementations of LISP interpreters, we have the following.

Convention 3: The empty list ( ) may be identified as the atom NIL.

This convention has profound consequences. Conventions 2 and 3 cause a 'semantic bottleneck' concerning NIL. NIL may be considered at the same time as

(1) some atom called NIL
(2) the empty list
(3) the logical value False.

   In fact, the atom NIL is whatever its context requires it to be. Its many meanings, avoiding changes of type, facilitate program writing and obscure the legibility of these programs only on rare occasions.

   Nevertheless it is very important to note that ( ) is no longer a list but an atom, since the value of (ATOM '( )) is T. This property is the source of numerous errors and therefore requires extra care when used.

■ Many LISP interpreters have a certain convention which may be viewed as a result of conventions 2 and 3:

As far as logic values are concerned, any LISP object apart from NIL, is considered as representing True

Thus T represents True (tt), and C6H5OH also represents True (tt), as does (ACID BASE ALDEHYDE) or 'T or even (NIL).

As we will be able to establish later on, this convention, which is more lax than convention 2, simplifies program writing to a large extent. Note, nevertheless, that this convention does not imply that the predicates encountered so far (NULL, EQ, ATOM) may have any object as their value (NIL or not-NIL): they only return the atom NIL or T as their value, T being a particular representative of the class of objects signifying True.

1.4 Historical Background

For reasons that are once again historical, the functions FIRST, REST and INSERT, which have already been mentioned, are better known by the less memorable names of CAR, CDR and CONS respectively.

CONS means CONStructing lists whilst CAR and CDR originate from 'Content of Address Register' and 'Content of Decrement Register' and are operations that are totally related to the first computer on which LISP was created.

Of course, it is always possible to define the functions FIRST, REST and INSERT, if they do not already exist, on any LISP interpreter that is in use today; however, as the names CAR, CDR and CONS are used world-wide, we will abandon the mnemonics FIRST, REST and INSERT. Therefore

(CAR '(ONE TWO THREE)) will yield the value ONE
(CDR '(FOUR FIVE))   will yield the value (FIVE)
(CONS 'ONE '(1))   will yield the value (ONE 1)

■ The names CAR and CDR, which differ only by a single letter, have led to a very useful convention. When you program in LISP, it is quite often necessary to write long sequences of CAR and CDR. If we recall the example where we wished to obtain the first term of the third term of a list, the sequence was

(CAR(CAR(CDR(CDR '((WE) (LOVE) (LISP))))))

This can be made more concise by writing

(CAADDR '((WE) (LOVE) (LISP)))

The atom CAADDR is therefore the name of the function

$car \circ car \circ cdr \circ cdr$

Hence

    (CADR '((WE) (LOVE) (LISP))) will yield the value (LOVE)
    (CDDDR '((WE) (LOVE) (LISP))) will yield the value NIL

Consequently, a combination of no CARs and no CDRs is denoted by CR:

    (CR '((WE) (LOVE) (LISP))) will yield the value ((WE) (LOVE) (LISP))

    CR is the identity function which it is important not to confuse with
QUOTE. Simply compare

    (CR(CONS 'T 'NIL))   which gives (T)

and

    (QUOTE(CONS 'T 'NIL)) which gives (CONS 'T 'NIL)

1.5 Exercises

1.5.1 Give the type (atom, list, program, badly structured expression) of the
following expressions:

        ATOM
        (LIS)P
        (L(I(S(P)))))
        (CAR(L I S P))
        (CONS 'CAR ''T)

1.5.2 What are the values of the following programs?

```
(CAR '(NIL))

(CDR '(ONE 2 III))

(CADR (CONS 'L '(I S P)))

(EQ 'T (ATOM 'NIL))

(NULL (NULL (ATOM '(NIL))))
```

2 First Steps in LISP

Whatever the type of computer being used (micro, mini or even mega) and whatever the way it requires to start the LISP interpreter, once loaded and about to execute, the interpreter will indicate its readiness in terms such as

LISP 1.5 IS WINNING AGAIN
?

The first line contains identification of the LISP being used and provides you with a customary welcome message. The question mark on the second line indicates that the interpreter is at your disposal from now on. These terms and the way of showing that LISP is waiting for a program from you are not universal to all existing interpreters; for example, some show their readiness to receive a program by printing EVAL: instead of a question mark. However, whatever method the computer uses to indicate its readiness, we can put it to the test, without further delay, by using the few programs that you already know how to write.

We shall use the following typographical convention: expressions will be input on lines commencing with a question mark, whereas the replies will be output, after a jump to the next line, starting in the fourth column (that is, preceded by three spaces). Note that there is no set format for replies either; for example, certain interpreters may print VALUE: before the reply.

Let us start then:

```
?(CAR '(A ROSE))
?   A
```

The reply is received immediately. The calculation is actually very simple since the atom A is the first term of the list (A ROSE). The question mark that then appears indicates that LISP is again ready to accept a new form.

```
?(CAR (CAR '((ONE) NIL)))
   ONE

?  (    CAAR   (QUOTE (
?  (  ONE
?           )()
?              ))
?)
   ONE

?         '
? ONE
   ONE
```

These last examples show that expressions input to LISP may be written in free format on one or several lines, and that any superfluous spaces have no effect on the interpreter. If there are not enough closing brackets, LISP will require these to be supplied on as many new lines as needed, each one commencing with a question mark.

Let us now continue by considering how to handle numbers:

```
?(+  1  2)
      3

?(+  1  2  3  4  5)
      15

?(*  2  (/  5  3)  (-  4  3))
      2

?(*  2  3.14159)
      6.28318
```

As there seems to be no flaw in LISP's arithmetic and computing capabilities, let us carry on with our tests:

```
?(SET  'P  3)
      3
```

Writing the program (SET 'P 3) is equivalent to writing the following assignment statement in BASIC:

LET P = 3

SET is a function that enables a value to be stored under a name, and will be studied in detail later on in section 3.7. The name appears as the first argument (that is, as the second term of the form) and the value as the second argument (that is, as the third term of the form). Then all you need do is use this name in order that the stored value be accessed and available for use: in this case, it would be said that the value of P is 3:

```
?P
      3

?(+  P  P)
      6

?(*  P  (+  P  1))
      12
```

Of course, variables may be redefined as shown in the following examples:

```
?(SET (QUOTE P) (* 2 P))
  6

?   P
  6

?(CAR (SET 'P (CONS P NIL)))
  6

?   P
  (6)

?(CAR (SET 'P '(CONS P NIL)))
  CONS

?   P
  (CONS P NIL)

?(SET (CADR P)(CADR P))
  P

?   P
  P
```

In a way, SET allows an atom to have a value. When you use LISP you will find that a certain number of atoms have already been defined, for example:

```
?   T
  T

?   NIL
  NIL
```

The atoms T and NIL have themselves as value. All the atoms representing the basic functions of the interpreter (CONS, CAR, CDR, NULL, EQ, ATOM, QUOTE, SET, as well as others) are also pre-defined. As far as these atoms are concerned, it is as if LISP itself evaluated the forms (SET 'T 'T) and (SET 'NIL 'NIL) before 'giving you control', in other words, before allowing you to enter expressions.

In the preceding examples, you will have noticed that the value of the form SET (the program whose first term is the atom SET) is that of its second argument. Unlike in BASIC, where only the value to be assigned is the result of a calculation, in LISP both the name of the variable and the value to be assigned to this variable may be calculated. This last point therefore justifies using the 'quote' (that is, the function QUOTE) in the assignments given as examples:

```
?(SET 'P 'Q)
    Q

?(SET P 3)
    3

?P
    Q

?Q
    3
```

Since the value of P is the atom Q, the second assignment corresponds to the
form (SET 'Q 3) which assigns the value 3 to the atom Q and changes neither
the atom P nor its value!

This concept of value is at the heart of LISP. When you enter a program
(a form or an atom), the LISP interpreter calculates its value which is then
printed on a new line: we say that it *evaluates* the expression. LISP evaluates
an atom by looking for the object that it stores. It evaluates a form by firstly
evaluating all the terms in the form and then applying the function (value of
the first term) to its arguments (values of terms one, two, three, etc.). But note
that this is true only in general terms, since we have already met an exception:
the function QUOTE which does not evaluate its argument but returns it as it is.
Later on we will see other functions of this same type.

The following, more detailed, example will clarify this fundamental concept
of evaluation. We will write a function which we will call FACT and which may
be used to calculate factorials. In mathematical terms: factorial (n) is written as
$n!$ and is defined as

$$n! = 1 \times 2 \times 3 \times \ldots \times (n - 1) \times n$$

This definition calls for the calculation to be done in a way that is
frequently used in other languages. In BASIC for example

```
LET FACT = 1
FOR I = 1 TO N
LET FACT = I * FACT
NEXT I
```

This is not the method we will use. Note that

$$n! = n \times (n - 1)!$$

and that

$$1! = 1$$

and therefore in LISP we write

```
?(DE FACT (N)
?   (IF (EQN N 1)
?      1
?         (* N (FACT (- N 1))) ) )
   FACT
```

We may translate this 'word for word' into English by the following. Definition (DE) of a function (called FACT), which has a single variable (called N), and which is defined as follows:

> If N is equal to 1 (EQN N 1)
> then the value of the function will be the constant 1
> else it is N times the value of factorial N—1

Such a function is said to be recursive as it appears in its own definition! We shall prove straight away that this type of situation does not cause any problems for our interpreter:

```
?(FACT 5)
   120

?(FACT (+ 6 7))
   6227020800
```

In order to explain the way in which LISP arrived at these results, let us evaluate the following form by hand, just as the interpreter would do it:

   ?(FACT 3)

In this example, the symbol ↑ will indicate the current position of the evaluation:

   (FACT 3)
   ↑

Having received a request to evaluate a program, LISP makes enquiries as to the nature of this program: atom or form? It is a list (hence a form), so LISP will evaluate the first term of this list in order to determine the function to be applied.

   (FACT 3)
      ↑

FACT is a known atom whose value is a function. LISP will therefore evaluate the argument of this function.

   (FACT 3)
         ↑

The argument is a number. A number is an atom that represents its own value, in this case, the integer number 3.

(FACT 3)
    ↑

There are no more arguments. We may therefore apply the function FACT to its argument: the number 3. This means calculating the following form for which the value of N will be 3 (we say: in the environment where N has the value 3).

(IF(EQN N 1) 1 (* N (FACT(-- N 1))))
↑

We continue with the evaluation by establishing the fact that we have a form whose first term will be evaluated.

(IF(EQN N 1) 1 (* N (FACT(– N 1))))
  ↑

The first term is the IF operator which necessitates the evaluation of its first argument and will, according to the returned logical value, force the evaluation of the second or third argument. It is thus necessary to evaluate the first argument.

(IF(EQN N 1) 1 (* N (FACT(– N 1))))
  ↑

It is a form whose first term

(IF(EQN N 1) 1 (* N (FACT(– N 1))))
   ↑

is a predicate testing equality between two numbers.

(IF(EQN N 1) 1 (* N (FACT(– N 1))))
    ↑ :

The first argument is N whose value, according to the current environment, is 3.

(IF(EQN 3 1) 1 (* N (FACT(– N 1))))
    ↑

The second argument is the constant 1.

(IF(EQN 3 1) 1 (* N (FACT(– N 1))))
    ↑

Having evaluated the two arguments of the predicate EQN, we may now apply this predicate, which returns False (that is, NIL) since 3 and 1 are different numbers.

(IF NIL 1 (∗ N(FACT(− N 1)))
 ↑

As the value of the first argument of IF is NIL, the value of the IF form will be the third argument. The second argument is therefore ignored and the evaluation will continue with the expression

(∗ N (FACT(− N 1)))
↑

which must be evaluated in the environment where the value of N is 3. It is a form whose first term is a well-known atom whose value is the multiplication function.

(∗ N(FACT(− N 1)))
  ↑

The second term or the first argument of the multiplication is the atom N whose value is 3 in this case.

(∗ 3 (FACT(− N 1)))
  ↑

The second argument is a form whose first term has the value of a known function: factorial.

(∗ 3 (FACT(− N 1)))
      ↑

We must therefore evaluate its argument which is once again a form whose value, in order to spare the details, is 2:

(∗ 3 (FACT 2))
       ↑

Having evaluated the FACT argument, we may now apply this function, which leads us to evaluate

(∗ 3 (IF(EQN N 1) 1 (∗ N (FACT(− N 1)))))
  ↑

But we must evaluate this form in the environment where the value of N is 2. Similar reasoning to that which has just been made would lead us to evaluate:

(∗ 3 (∗ 2 (FACT 1)))
         ↑

In other words

(∗ 3 (∗ 2 (IF (EQN N 1) 1 (∗ N (FACT(− N 1))))))
      ↑

in the environment where the value of N is 1. By following the rules associated with the IF operator, we will evaluate the first argument whose value, in this case, is T (that is, True): hence the value of the IF form will be the constant 1 and the result leads to the evaluation of

```
(* 3 (* 2 1))
       ↑
```

By applying the multiplication function to its two arguments, we arrive at

```
(* 3 2)
     ↑
```

By multiplying once again, the evaluation concludes with the answer:

```
6
```

which was the expected final result.

Without going into great detail, this example gives a basic idea of the LISP method of evaluation. It is important to remember that this method examines the forms from left to right and always evaluates the first term of the forms to start with, in order to deduce the function to be applied to the other terms of the form (which are not evaluated for QUOTE, which are evaluated in a certain order for IF, and which are all evaluated for other functions such as EQN, +, * or even FACT).

2.1 Exercises

2.1.1 Calculate

```
(FACT (FACT 2))

(FACT -1)
```

2.1.2 We define the factorial function in a different way, as follows:

```
(DE FACT (N)
   (IF (EQN N 1)
       1
       (* (FACT (- N 1)) N) ) )
```

Calculate

```
(FACT 3)
```

2.1.3 What is the purpose of the function defined below?

```
(DE UNKNOWN (L)
    (IF (ATOM L)
        L
        (UNKNOWN (CAR L)) ) )
    UNKNOWN
```

If in any doubt, calculate:

```
(UNKNOWN '(((ATOM AND OTHER THINGS)
             WITHOUT)
            ANY IMPORTANCE) )
```

3 Micro-manual

There is no recognised standard for LISP: each interpreter is written to contain the facilities desired by its author and, consequently, this book is itself biased. Nevertheless, certain functions are standard and these will be found in all interpreters. We will examine this basic core in detail, while pointing out the most general characteristics of existing interpreters. In this book we have used a 'pure' LISP, which excludes most of the characteristics that are particular to any single 'dialect'. The LISP to which we will introduce you is described in LISP itself in the Appendix. If you are familiar with another dialect, this definition will enable you to grasp the characteristics of the one used here, or if you have a LISP interpreter at your disposal, you can simulate the one in this book, without any error, by means of the definition that we provide. This carefully written definition works on any interpreter, with no need for modification. Having two interpreters at your disposal (one belonging to the system, the other simulated) you will be able to combine the better characteristics of the two, and thus create your own dialect.

This chapter deals therefore with the main LISP functions. Instead of discussing how to use some 50–150 generally available functions, we will introduce only the minimum number. As LISP is a universal language, these conditions can easily be accepted, since it is possible to write the functions that we will omit.

For each function, we will give:

(1) the way in which it is called
(2) the nature of its arguments
(3) its result
(4) examples, remarks and other comments on its use.

To assist further the understanding of the order and meaning of the arguments, we will use the following convention:

(IF *if then else* . . .) represents the way of calling the conditional form IF

The first argument will be known by the name *if*
The second by the name *then*
The third and following by the name *else* . . . (the three dots indicate the possibility of several expressions being present)

Thus, for the call

(IF (LE N 1) 1 (∗ N (FACT (− N 1))))

the part corresponding to *if* will be the form (LE N 1) the *then* part will be the constant 1, whilst the *else* . . . part will correspond to the single form (∗ N (FACT (− N 1))).

In order to make this chapter comprehensive, we will briefly revise the functions that have already been described.

3.1 Basic Functions

■ (CAR *expression*)

Argument: The value of *expression* must be a non-empty list.
Value: The first term of the non-empty list that is the value of *expression*.

Example

```
?(CAR '(THIS IS A LIST))
   THIS
```

■ (CDR *expression*)

Argument: The value of *expression* must be a non-empty list.
Value: The entire list (that is, the value of *expression*) with its first term
             omitted.

Examples

```
?(CDR '(LIST NOT EMPTY))
   (NOT EMPTY)

?(CDR '(LIST))
   NIL
```

Notes on CAR and CDR
When the value of *expression* is an object other than a non-empty list, the interpreter displays an error message in appropriate terms: for example

∗∗∗∗∗ INCORRECT-FORM : (CAR *expression*)

Nevertheless, certain interpreters adopt a further convention (not assumed in this book) that the value of (CAR NIL) and (CDR NIL) is NIL. The decision whether or not to include this convention as a facility is left to the reader's judgement.

■ (CONS *expression list*)

Arguments: *expression* may have any value, the value of *list* on the other hand,
            must be either a non-empty list or the atom NIL.
Value: A new list whose first term is the value of *expression* and whose
            following terms are those contained in the value of *list*.

Examples

```
?(CONS 'LIST 'NIL)
   (LIST)

?(CONS '(CONS ALWAYS RETURNS A)
?        '(LIST) )
   ((CONS ALWAYS RETURNS A) LIST)
```

Notes

When the value of *list* is an object that is not a list (empty or not), the interpreter will not display an error, but will form an unusual object called a dotted
pair. Dotted pairs will be analysed and discussed in greater detail in chapter 8.

```
?(CONS 'DOTTED 'PAIR)
   (DOTTED . PAIR)
```

Dotted pairs are survivors of an earlier stage of the language, derived from
the dot that separates their two components: the CAR part and the CDR part.

■ (ATOM *expression*)

Argument: *expression* may have any value.
Value: ATOM is a predicate returning a value of T or NIL depending on
          whether the value of *expression* is an atom or not.

Example

```
?(ATOM 'ATOM)
   T

?(ATOM NIL)
   T

?(ATOM (+ 1 2))
   T

?(ATOM '(NOT EMPTY LIST))
   NIL
```

Note

Atoms were introduced in chapter 1 as indivisible objects represented by a
sequence of contiguous characters. Atoms whose name consists purely of

figures are numbers that may be used freely by arithmetic operators. By convention, any object that is not a non-empty list, in other words, that has not been built by CONS, is an atom. This convention allows the following program:

```
?(ATOM ATOM)
   T
```

Therefore functions are atoms!

More formally, we define the collection of atoms (*ATOM*) as the combination of three separate sub-units.

> *NUMBER:*   All integer numbers ($\ldots -1, 0, +1 \ldots$).
> *FUNCTION:*   All functions (*null, atom, fact* ...).
> *ID:*   All identifiers, that is, all atoms that are neither
>   numbers nor functions (ATOM, NULL, C6H5OH. . .)

We write

> *ATOM = NUMBER ∪ FUNCTION ∪ ID*

Later on we will see that the predicates NUMBERP, FUNCTIONP and IDP may be used to discriminate between atoms.

Functions are very special objects that are represented and handled in various ways by LISP interpreters (this being one of the basic points where LISP interpreters differ). In actual fact, a function is not a real identifier.

```
?(DE LOGARITHM (N)
?    (IF (LE N 1)
?       1
?          (* N (LOGARITHM (- N 1))) ) )
     LOGARITHM
```

This program defines a LISP function called LOGARITHM which calculates the mathematical function known as factorial!

Most of the time a function exists only because there is an identifier that gives it a name, the value of this identifier being the function. DE builds a function by giving it a name, but later on we will see how to build anonymous functions.

In chapter 1 we carefully distinguished between *car* and the identifier CAR. When we write

```
?(ATOM CAR)
   T
```

the question arises whether the value of the identifier CAR is an atom or not; in other words, whether the object that we call *car* is an atom or not, assuming that the user has not altered CAR. Conventionally the reply is yes.

We may therefore write

```
?(ATOM LOGARITHM)
   T
```

and obtain the desired result.

This convention is quite simple (what is the first term of a function?) and means that we can apply the functions CAR or CDR, without running any risks, to objects that return the value NIL to the predicate ATOM.

■ (EQ *expression 1 expression 2*)

Arguments: *expression 1* and *expression 2* may have any value.
Value: EQ is a predicate that returns the value T or NIL according to whether the values of *expression 1* and *expression 2* are the same atom or not.

Example

```
?(EQ 'ATOM 'LIST)
   NIL

?(EQ 'ATOM (CAR '(ATOM 'ATOM)))
   T

?(EQ (+ 1 2) (- 4 1))
   T

?(EQ ATOM ATOM)
   T
```

Note

In many dialects, equality between two numbers is tested by a special predicate (EQN) and not by EQ as is the case here. The value of EQN is True (T) if, and only if, its two arguments are equal numbers, otherwise its value is NIL.

If, with your interpreter, EQ may not be applied to numbers, you can redefine EQ as

```
?(PROGN (SET 'OLD-EQ EQ) ; keep eq
?          (DE EQ (E1 E2)
?             (OR (OLD-EQ E1 E2)
?                 (EQN E1 E2) ) ) )
   EQ

?(EQ 1 (+ 1 0))
   T
```

The former function EQ is now the value of identifier OLD-EQ which means that EQ may be restored to its initial value if so desired. Without taking this precaution, the function *eq* would have been lost as it would be inaccessible:

furthermore, no identifier would have this function as its value and, as it is a basic function, we would not be able to recreate it in LISP.

- (NULL *expression*)

Argument: *expression* may have any value.

Value: NULL is a predicate that returns the value T or NIL according to whether the value of *expression* is the empty list (the atom NIL) or not.

Example

```
?(NULL T)
   NIL

?(NULL (CDR '(LIST)))
   T
```

Note

NULL is not one of LISP's primitive functions and may therefore be defined as:

```
?(DE NULL (EXP)
?    (EQ EXP NIL) )
   NULL
```

With regard to logic values (see section 1.3.2), NULL behaves like the negation function called NOT, which is defined as

```
?(DE NOT (EXP)
?    (EQ EXP NIL) )
   NOT
```

Of course, we get

```
?(NOT T)
   NIL

?(NOT NIL)
   T
```

- (CONSP *expression*)

Argument: *expression* may have any value.

Value: CONSP is a predicate that returns the value T or NIL according to whether the value of *expression* is a non-empty list or not.

Example

```
?(CONSP '(LIST))
   T

?(CONSP ATOM)
   NIL

?(CONSP 314)
   NIL

?(CONSP 'ATOM)
   NIL
```

Note

CONSP is the predicate that complements **ATOM** and which we define as

```
?(DE CONSP (EXP)
?   (NOT (ATOM EXP)) )
   CONSP
```

■ (IDP *expression*)

Argument: *expression* may have any value.
Value: IDP is a predicate returning T or NIL depending on whether the
            value of *expression* is an identifier or not.

Example

```
?(IDP 'ABCDEF)
   T
?(IDP (+ 2 3))
   NIL
```

Note

IDP may be considered as a sub-predicate of ATOM since any expression that
satisfies IDP will also satisfy ATOM. IDP is sometimes known as SYMBOLP,
the identifiers being referred to as 'atomic symbols'.

■ (IF *if then else* . . .)

Arguments: *if* and *then* are any two forms.
            else . . . is a sequence of forms which may even be omitted.
Value: Firstly the interpreter evaluates the *if* form. If the value of *if* is
            different to NIL, in other words, if it corresponds to the logic
            value True, then the value of the *then* form will be fetched,
            otherwise we fetch the value of (PROGN *else* . . .). PROGN is
            explained later.

Examples

```
?(IF T 1 2)
   1

?(IF NIL 1 2)
   2

?(IF (NULL '(LIST)) 1
?     2 3 4 5 )
   5

?(IF (NOT T) T)
   NIL
```

Note

IF is the basic conditional expression which, along with the predicates, allows us to control the evaluation so as to apply the correct operators to the correct arguments. For example

```
?(SET 'A-LIST '(3 1 4 1 5 9 2))
   (3 1 4 1 5 9 2)

?(IF (CONSP A-LIST)
?     (CAR A-LIST)
?     (+ 1 A-LIST) )
   3

?(SET 'A-LIST (CAR A-LIST))
   3

?(IF (CONSP A-LIST)(CAR A-LIST)
?     (+ 1 A-LIST) )
   4
```

■ (PROGN *forms* . . .)

Argument: *forms* . . . is any sequence of forms.

Value: PROGN evaluates its arguments in order. The value of the last argument is the value of PROGN. By convention, the value of (PROGN) is NIL.

Example

```
?(PROGN 1 2 3)
   3

?(PROGN 1 2)
   2
```

```
? ( PROGN 1 )
    1

? ( IF ( NOT T ) 1 )
    NIL
```

Note

PROGN is only beneficial to functions that cause side-effects (for example, SET, DE, PRINT, READ, etc.). Generally, functions are characterised by their value, but occasionally they produce lasting effects which affect the sequence of evaluations: they are therefore considered to produce side-effects. For example

```
? ( SET 'N ( + 2 ( SET 'P 1 ) ) )
    3

? N
    3

? P
    1
```

Although the value of (SET 'P 1) is 1 (this value being added to 2 to become the value of the identifier N), the basic and essential side-effect is the association of the value 1 with the atom P.

There is no point in writing the form

```
? ( PROGN ( + 1 2 3 4 )
?          ( CDR ' ( LIST ) )
?          ( NOT NIL ) )
    T
```

as we get the same result as if we had written

```
? ( PROGN ( NOT NIL ) )
    T
```

since we gained nothing from the successive evaluation of (+ 1 2 3 4) and (CDR '(LIST))! On the other hand

```
? ( PROGN ( SET 'N ( + N 1 ) )
?          ' INCREMENT )
    INCREMENT
```

allows us to increment the variable N and to return a constant value.

■ (QUOTE *expression*)

Argument: *expression* is some object.

Value: The value of the form (QUOTE *expression*) is *expression*. This function is by no means trivial and must not be confused with the identity function.

Example

```
?(QUOTE QUOTE)
   QUOTE

?(QUOTE 'ATOM)
   (QUOTE ATOM)

?(QUOTE (* 1 2 3))
   (* 1 2 3)
```

Note

The Identity function is defined as

```
?(DE IDENTITY (EXP)
?   EXP )
   IDENTITY
```

By using this function we arrive at

```
?(IDENTITY 'ATOM)
   ATOM

?(IDENTITY (* 1 2 3))
   6
```

The Identity function is also known as CR (see section 1.4).

As the atoms T and NIL have themselves as value, there is no need to 'QUOTE' them when they are used.

```
?(EQ NIL 'NIL)
   T

?(EQ T 'T)
   T
```

This is the same for numbers that also have themselves as value:

```
?(EQ 3 (QUOTE 3))
   T
```

Do not forget that *'expression* is a quick, convenient and useful abbreviation
for (QUOTE *expression*).

■ (EVAL *expression*)

Argument: The value of *expression* may be any object.

Value: The value of this form will be the value of the value of *expression*.
If the value of *expression* is a non-empty list, then the returned
value will be the value of this list, which is considered to be a form.
If the value of *expression* is an atom, then either it is an identifier,
in which case the result will be the value of this identifier, or it is a
number or a function and, by convention, the returned value will
be this number or this function.

Examples

```
?(EVAL T)
   T

?(PROGN (SET 'N '(+ 1 2))
?        (EVAL N) )
   3

?(EVAL (EVAL N))
   3

?(EVAL (QUOTE (+ 1 2)))
   3

?(EVAL (QUOTE (QUOTE (+ 1 2))))
   (+ 1 2)
```

Note

The main purpose of EVAL is to turn a list into a form and hence calculate its
value. Since we know how to build lists, and therefore programs, by using
CONS, we can now use EVAL to evaluate (that is, execute) them. Thus

```
?(EVAL (CONS 'CAR
?            (CONS (CONS 'QUOTE
?                       (CONS '(NOT
?                               EMPTY
?                               LIST )
?                             NIL ))
?                 NIL )))
   NOT
```

The first argument of EVAL is a form that builds the program
(CAR '(NON EMPTY LIST)) and EVAL executes it.

With regard to EVAL, QUOTE acts as a sort of reciprocal function, since we may always replace the form (EVAL (QUOTE *expression*)) by *expression*.

The function EVAL condenses a LISP system entirely since, like the system, it takes a list on input and returns its value on output. However, the behaviour of the LISP system may be represented by the function TOPLEVEL defined as

```
?(DE TOPLEVEL ()
?    (PRINT (EVAL (READ)))
?    (TOPLEVEL) )
     TOPLEVEL
```

which indicates that the interpreter reads an expression, evaluates it, prints its result and starts again.

If only we could write EVAL in LISP we would have a definition of LISP in LISP. This is possible, and such a function will be shown in the Appendix.

The function EVAL is one of the most noticeable characteristics of LISP, which distinguishes it from other languages. You will see many uses of it in section 3.7 when we deal with special functions.

3.2 Exercises

3.2.1 Evaluate

```
(EQ (CONS (CAR '(LIST))
          (CDR '(LIST)) )
    '(LIST) )

(CDR (CONS CONS '(('LIST NIL)))

(EVAL (CONS CONS '(('LIST NIL)))
```

3.2.2 What does the following function do?

```
(DE SPRING-WATER (EXP)
   (IF (NULL EXP)
       T
       NIL ) )
```

3.2.3 Write a function that returns the type of its argument: that is, LIST if it is a list, ATOM if it is an atom.

3.2.4 Write a test function. The value of the atom PROGS is a list of forms to test. The call (TEST) evaluates the first program in this list and removes it.

3.3 Dealing with Numbers in LISP

Though qualified as a symbolic language, in other words, it is able to handle symbols, LISP also has an equal knowledge of everyday arithmetic facilities. In this section, we will limit ourselves to signed integer numbers ($\ldots, -2, -1, 0, +1, +2, \ldots$) although, generally, interpreters also allow 'real' numbers (such as $3.1415926\ldots, 2.718282\ldots$).

An interesting point is that a certain number of interpreters currently on the market allow for multi-precision; in other words, any integer number, whatever it is, may be stored so far as your memory constraints allow, without you having to specify anything. It is completely automatic. You can write for example

```
?(FACT 20)
2432902008176640000
```

As we saw above, numbers are special atoms that have themselves as value:

```
?-121
-121
```

On the other hand we cannot write

```
?(SET 12 13)
*****FIRST-ARGUMENT-IS-NOT-A-SYMBOL:12
```

since, of course, each number has its own distinct value. The conventions used to write arithmetic expressions are the usual LISP conventions. Let us refresh our memory: any operation is represented by a list whose first term is the name of the function to be applied (the operator) and whose other terms are the operands of the function. Thus

$$3 + 4 \qquad \text{will be written as } (+\ 3\ 4)$$
$$3 + (4 \times 2) \qquad \text{will be written as } (+\ 3\ (*\ 4\ 2))$$
$$(3 + 4) \times 2 \qquad \text{will be written as } (*\ (+\ 3\ 4)\ 2)$$
$$\frac{1}{\sqrt{(2\pi n)}} \left(\frac{n}{e}\right)^n \text{ will be written as } (\ /\ (\text{EXP}\ (/\ N\ E)N)$$
$$(\text{SQRT}(*\ 2$$
$$\text{PI}$$
$$N))\ )$$

having suitably initialised E and PI.

This notation is clumsy and is not as elegant as the mathematical representation. Nevertheless, it is simple to write a function in LISP itself, which translates arithmetic expressions from BASIC notation to LISP notation, as well as the other way round. We could, for example, write

```
?(BASIC-TO-LISP '(A * X ↑ 2 + B * X + C))
   (+ (* A (↑ X 2)) (+ (* B X) C))

?(EVAL (BASIC-TO-LISP '(A * X ↑ 2 + B * X + C)))
```

As we see, it is one of LISP's qualities that a program may be executed or analysed by a second program which will alter and improve it to produce, for example, a third program which itself may be executed or analysed. Here for example, the program is written according to the conventions of its writer, translated (through the evaluation of a translation form) to give a normal LISP expression, and then evaluated.

We will present the functions one after another as we did in the previous section, and will point out the important characteristics of each one. We will conclude this section by giving a few examples of quite common complementary functions. All the arithmetic functions evaluate their arguments and all of them have a fixed number of arguments, apart from PLUS and TIMES.

■ (NUMBERP *expression*)

Argument: *expression* may have any value.
Value: NUMBERP is a predicate that returns the value T or NIL,
           according to whether the value of *expression* is a number or not.

Example

```
?(NUMBERP 3)
    T

?(NUMBERP (+ 3 4))
    T

?(DE FACT (E)
?   (IF (NUMBERP E)
?       (IF (LE E 1) 1
?           (EVAL (BASIC-TO-LISP '(E * FACT (E - 1))))  )
?       'FOOLISH ) )
    FACT
```

Note

NUMBERP allows numbers to be recognised as such, which means that in the last example, FACT is applied only when it makes sense. Generally, it is in your interest to protect your functions by making them test the nature of their arguments before any calculation. You may also rely on the interpreter's abilities (which vary a great deal depending on the one you use) to perform tests and to allow these types of error to be corrected, for example

```
?(/ (+ 1 'A) 2)
*****ERRONEOUS-FORM:(+ 1 (QUOTE A))
***VALUE-OF-FORM?
?(PROGN (PRINT (LIST 'A '= A))
?         (+ 1 A) )
(A := 7)
   4
```

The exact explanation of this error recovery will be given in chapter 9.

■ (PLUS *numbers...*)

Argument: *numbers...* is a sequence of expressions whose values must be
          numerical.
Value: The sum of the values of the expressions present in *numbers...*
          By convention the value of (PLUS) is zero.

Example

```
?(+ (SET 'N -1) (PLUS N N) (PLUS))
  -3
```

Notes
The function PLUS is often abbreviated to the symbol '+', in other words, at
the initialisation stage, LISP evaluated (SET '+ PLUS) which means we have
the same function (addition) under two different names.
    Note also that PLUS takes any number of arguments and evaluates them all.
    The following function will be found in any self-respecting LISP interpreter:

```
?(DE ADD1 (N)
?   (PLUS N 1) )
   ADD1
```

■ (DIFFERENCE *number 1 number 2*)

Argument: The values of *number 1* and *number 2* must be numbers.
Value: The value of *number 2* subtracted from that of *number 1*.

Example

```
?(DIFFERENCE 1968 (ADD1 1066))
  901
```

Notes
The function DIFFERENCE is also abbreviated to '−'. As with ADD1, the
function SUB1 also exists and is defined as

```
?(DE SUB1 (N)
?    (- N 1) )
     SUB1
```

There is a function derived from DIFFERENCE, which gives the opposite of an integer number:

```
?(DE MINUS (N)
?    (- 0 N) )
     MINUS

?(MINUS -1981)
     1981
```

- (TIMES *numbers...*)

Arguments: *numbers...* is a sequence of expressions whose values must be numerical.

Value: The number produced by multiplying the values of the expressions present in *numbers...* By convention, the value of (TIMES) is 1.

Example

```
?(TIMES (SET 'N -1) (MINUS N))
     -1
```

Notes
The function TIMES is also abbreviated to '*'. As with the function PLUS, TIMES deals with any number of evaluated arguments.

- (QUOTIENT *number 1 number 2*)

Arguments: The values of *number 1* and *number 2* must be numerical.
Value: The quotient of the value of *number 1* divided by that of *number 2*.

Example

```
?(QUOTIENT +26 (ADD1 7))
     3
```

Note
QUOTIENT is often abbreviated to '/'.

- (REMAINDER *number 1 number 2*)

Arguments: The values of *number 1* and *number 2* must be numerical.

Value: The remainder after dividing the value of *number 1* by the
                value of *number 2*.

Example

```
?(EQ (SET 'N 1984)
?      (+ (* (/ N 31) 31)
?          (REMAINDER N 31) ) )
   T
```

Notes

REMAINDER is often abbreviated to 'MOD'.

   If we wish to obtain the quotient and remainder by using a single function,
we define for example

```
?(DE DIVIDE (N P)
?   (CONS (/ N P)
?          (CONS (MOD N P) NIL) ) )
   DIVIDE

?(DIVIDE 10001 237)
   (42 47)
```

■ The functions +, −, *, /, MOD are all that is required in order to perform
arithmetical operations, but nevertheless we must at least add a few predicates
that can be used for comparisons, in order to be able to write more interesting
functions. Some examples of these now follow.

■ (GREATERP *number 1 number 2*)

Arguments: The values of *number 1* and *number 2* must be numerical.
Value: GREATERP is a predicate that returns the value T or NIL
            according to whether the value of *number 1* is strictly greater
            than the value of *number 2* or not.

Example

```
?(GREATERP 1 (MINUS 1))
   T

?(GREATERP 0 0)
   NIL
```

Notes

GREATERP is often abbreviated to 'GT' (as in FORTRAN).

   All other predicates may be defined by using EQN and GREATERP as
their starting point. If you do not have EQN, the definition will be as follows:

```
?(DE EQN (N P)
?    (AND (NUMBERP N)
?          (NUMBERP P)
?          (EQ N P) ) )
     EQN
```

We will also define:

```
?(DE ZEROP (N)
?    (EQ N 0) )
     ZEROP

?(DE MINUSP (N)
?    (GT 0 N) )
     MINUSP
```

You will note that most of the predicates in LISP end with the letter 'P' (for predicate) except, unfortunately, for the ones used most often: ATOM, NULL, EQ, etc. (this is due once again to historical influences). Other predicates used for comparisons may supplement the collection of arithmetic predicates.

```
?(DE GE (N P)
?    (NOT (LT N P)) )
     GE

?(DE LE (N P)
?    (NOT (GT N P)) )
     LE

?(DE LT (N P)
?    (GT P N) )
     LT
```

LT is often known as LESSP.

■ Examples of functions

It may seem as though some functions are missing (for example the exponentiation or the square root); let us prove that from now on it is possible to write them.

■ (EXP *number power*)

We will write:

```
?(DE EXP (N P)
?   (IF (LE P 0) 1
?       (IF (ZEROP (MOD P 2))
?           (EXP (SQUARE N) (/ P 2))
?           (* N (EXP N (SUB1 P))) ) ) )
    EXP
```

The exponentiation uses the following function which returns the square of its argument.

```
?(DE SQUARE (N)
?   (TIMES N N) )
    SQUARE
```

The programming of the function EXP is based on the following relations:

$$\forall\, p > 0 \quad n^{2p} = (n^2)^p$$

and

$$\forall\, p \geqslant 0 \quad n^{2p+1} = n(n^{2p})$$

the termination case is $n^0 = 1$.

Notice that we test (LE P 0) and not (EQN P 0), so that we protect ourselves from a negative power which would lead to an infinite calculation (see exercise 2.1.1).

As it contains fewer multiplications, this method is a lot quicker than the following one which involves multiplying N by itself P times:

```
?(DE EXP (N P)
?   (IF (LE P 0) 1
?       (* N (EXP N (SUB1 P))) ) )
    EXP
```

Examples

Suppose that we wish to evaluate (EXP 7 (ADD1 4)) and that we have opted to 'trace' (that is, to write down) all the calls to the functions EXP and SQUARE (see chapter 9). This gives us

```
?(TRACE EXP SQUARE)
    (EXP SQUARE)

?(EXP 7 (ADD1 4))
(EXP 7 5)
  (EXP 7 4)
  (SQUARE 7)
49
```

```
   (EXP 49 2)
 (SQUARE 49)
2401
   (EXP 2401 1)
    (EXP 2401 0)
    1
   2401
  2401
 2401
16807
   16807
```

■ (SQRT *number*)

We suggest the following definition:

```
?(DE SQRT (N)
?  (SQRT1 1) )
   SQRT

?(DE SQRT1 (P)
?  (IF (GT (* P P) N)
?       (SUB1 P)
?       (SQRT1 (ADD1 P)) ) )
   SQRT1

?(SQRT  51)
   7
```

We leave it to the reader to invent quicker methods than the one suggested above, whose equivalent in BASIC is:

```
100 REM SUB-PROGRAM SQRT
101 REM ARGUMENT IN N
102 REM RESULT IN S
110 LET S = 1
120 IF S * S ⩾ N THEN GOTO 150
130 LET S = S + 1
140 GOTO 120
150 LET S = S − 1
160 RETURN
```

The function SQRT1 corresponds to lines 120 to 160.

3.4 Exercises

3.4.1 Write the LISP expression that calculates

(a) the golden section $\dfrac{1 + \sqrt{5}}{2}$

(b) the single term $\dfrac{x^n}{n!}$

3.4.2 Define the function C that calculates

$$\binom{n}{p}$$

In other words, the number of distinct groups of p objects that you can extract from n. Use

$$\binom{n}{p} = \frac{n!}{p!\,(n-p)!}$$

or

$$\binom{n}{p} = \binom{n-1}{p-1} + \binom{n-1}{p}$$

with

$$\binom{n}{0} = 1$$

$$\binom{n}{n} = 1$$

3.4.3 Let the sequence for positive numbers be defined by:

$$\text{if } U_n \text{ is even then } U_{n+1} = \frac{U_n}{2}$$

$$\text{if } U_n \text{ is odd then } U_{n+1} = 3U_n + 1$$

Write a function whose argument is U_0 and which returns on exit the list of successive values of U_n up until the value 1; for example

(SEQUENCE 6) will have the value (6 3 10 5 16 8 4 2 1)

3.5 Input/Output

There are a few, simple functions that enable the transfer of information from the user to the LISP interpreter and vice versa. We will give only the two main ones here, but in chapter 9 we will add some special functions which allow more detailed control over printing.

The aim of the input/output functions is to convert LISP objects into character sequences and vice versa. The main functions are called PRINT and READ.

■ (PRINT *expression*)

Argument: The value of *expression* must be a list or a number or an identifier.
Value: The value of this form is the value of *expression*, the main purpose
          of this function being to print the value of *expression* (or to display
          it on a screen). Once this object has been printed (or displayed) the
          interpreter automatically goes to a new line.

Examples

```
?(PROGN (PRINT (CONS 'TESTING '(PRINT)))
?       T )
(TESTING PRINT)
    T
?(PRINT (PRINT 'PRINT-NEW-LINE))
PRINT-NEW-LINE
PRINT-NEW-LINE
    PRINT-NEW-LINE
```

Notes

Notice that the atom PRINT-NEW-LINE is printed three times. There are, in
effect, two calls to PRINT, therefore the atom concerned is printed twice at
the beginning of the line (with an automatic new line after each print). Finally,
the value returned by the initial form is this same atom, which is therefore
printed once again (but this time with three spaces preceding it, as is the case
with all values of expressions input to the interpreter).

If you insert printing instructions in function definitions, then PRINT
allows you to trace functions. For example, let us redefine factorial:

```
?(DE FACT (N)
?   (PRINT (CONS 'FACT (CONS N NIL)))
?   (CADDDR (PRINT (CONS 'FACT
?                   (CONS N
?                   (CONS '=
?                   (CONS (IF (LE N 1) 1
?                             (* N (FACT (SUB1 N))) )
?                   NIL ) ) ) ))) )
    FACT

?(FACT 6)
(FACT 6)
(FACT 5)
(FACT 4)
(FACT 3)
(FACT 2)
(FACT 1)
(FACT 1 = 1)
(FACT 2 = 2)
(FACT 3 = 6)
```

```
(FACT  4  =  24)
(FACT  5  =  120)
(FACT  6  =  720)
   720
```

Although generating many lines containing only moderately informative
details we have, nevertheless, a means by which we may follow the sequence
of evaluations. (In chapter 9 we will discuss some functions that enable functions
to be traced, altering their definition by automatically carrying out what we did
by hand.)

■ (READ)

Argument: None
Value: READ requests a LISP expression which it reads and returns as value.

Example

```
?(PROGN (PRINT '(VALUE OF EXPRESSION))
?        (SET 'EXP (READ))
?        (PRINT 'THANKS)
?        T )
(VALUE OF EXPRESSION)
?    (THAT LIST WILL
?        BE READ     )
THANKS
    T

?EXP
    (THAT LIST WILL BE READ)
```

Notes
The expression that is read is not evaluated and therefore has no need to be
QUOTED.

We are able to insert comments in LISP. These comments are ignored by the
reading process. A comment starts with the symbol ';', and finishes at the end
of the line (this is by far the commonest convention).

Example

```
?(DE TOPLEVEL ()       ; verbose toplevel loop
?  (PRINT 'EVAL:)
?  (PRINT (PROG1 (EVAL (READ))
?                    (PRINT 'VALUE:) ))
?  (IF (PROGN (PRINT 'CONTINUE:)
?             (READ) )   ; answer t to continue
?      (TOPLEVEL)
?      (PRINT 'END:)
?      (EVAL (READ)) ) )    ; final value
    TOPLEVEL
```

```
?(FACT (READ))   ; not giving a number
?ATOM            ; causes an error in fact
*****ERRONEOUS-FORM:(LE N 1)
***VALUE-OF-FORM?
?(TOPLEVEL)      ; inspect the environment
EVAL:
?N               ; value of n ?
VALUE:
ATOM
CONTINUE:
?T               ; let us continue
EVAL:
?(SET 'N 6)      ; change value of n
VALUE:
6
CONTINUE:
?NIL             ; exit from loop
END:
?NIL             ; and set the final value of toplevel
     720         ; which becomes that of (le n 0)
```

The calculation has continued without any error and has given the correct result. This example shows us how we can use PRINT and READ in a simple way, to produce a small evaluator that allows environmental errors to be corrected.

PRINT produces a straightforward print. For example:

```
?(PRINT '(PROGN (DE FACT (N)
?                  (IF (ZEROP N)
?                       1
?                      (* (FACT (SUB1 N)) N) ) )
?               (DE TOPLEVEL ()
?                  (PRINT (EVAL (READ)))
?                  (TOPLEVEL) ) ))
  (PROGN (DE FACT (N) (IF (ZEROP N) 1 (* (FACT (SUB1 N))
  N))) (DE TOPLEVEL NIL (PRINT (EVAL (READ))) (TOPLEVEL)
  ))
```

This form of printing is not easy to read and totally justifies the following acronym of LISP: 'Lot of Insipid and Stupid Parentheses'. All the LISP expressions in this book are laid out according to a certain number of rules for alignment and indentation (for example, arguments belonging to the same form are often written in columns, closing brackets that correspond to opening brackets on a same line are printed with no intermediate space). We can write a function in LISP that provides us with this improved printing. This function is commonly known as PRETTY-PRINT.

When reading this chapter, functions will appear to be 'unnamable' objects since they cannot be printed. What, in fact, can we associate with a function? Perhaps its name (although it may not even have one), or its definition (which always exists); but in the latter case we cannot distinguish the function from the list (that is, the form) defining it. We have therefore to admit that functions are objects that can be created in LISP, but for which there is no simple equivalent as far as character sequences are concerned. Hence

```
?( (PRINT CAR) '(PRINT RETURNS THE FUNCTION
?                    NEVERTHELESS ) )
***UNPRINTABLE-OBJECT
   PRINT
```

An error is reported but the value of CAR is correctly applied to the inserted form; that is, in all cases, whether the argument is printable or not, the value of (PRINT *expression*) is the value of *expression*.

3.6 Exercises

3.6.1 What value will be printed by:

```
(PRINT (+ 2 3))

(PRINT '(+ 2 3))

(PRINT (CONS (READ) (READ))) A (B)
```

3.6.2 Write a function that prints all the terms of its single argument one after another. Its value will always be NIL. For example

```
?(LPRINT '(A AB ABC))
A
AB
ABC
    NIL
```

3.7 Functions

This section will conclude this micro-manual. Functions are by far the most useful objects in LISP. It is by using functions that a user may build his program. Functions are identified by a definition made up of a list of variables and a 'body' that shows how to calculate the value of this function. Generally, this body uses variables, present in its list of variables, whose values are the arguments used when calling the function.

3.7.1 Different types of function

Let us sum up the types of function that we have already met. One class consists of the functions EQ, CONS, CAR, CDR, CONSP, SYMBOLP, NUMBERP, DIFFERENCE, QUOTIENT, REMAINDER, PRINT, READ, etc. These functions are concerned with the value of their arguments, of which there is a fixed number. We say that these functions are of the type SUBR (for 'subroutine'). They are generally primitive functions which cannot be defined in LISP.

A second class comprises the functions ATOM, NULL, INSERT, FIRST, REST, LE, LT, GT, ADD1, SUB1, FACT, TOPLEVEL, UNKNOWN, SPRING-WATER, etc. As with the SUBR, these functions are concerned with the value of their arguments of which there is a fixed number. Their only difference is that they are defined in LISP itself (usually by using DE). These functions are said to be of the type EXPR (for 'Expression').

We have been briefly introduced to two other function classes. The third class is made up of the functions TIMES and PLUS (as well as + and *) which are concerned with the value of their arguments of which there may be any number. If they were defined in LISP, they would be said to be of type NEXPR. As they are primitive in our case, we will say they are of type NSUBR (we have not as yet given an example of a function of type NEXPR).

The fourth class comprises the functions QUOTE, PROGN, IF and DE, which are not interested in the value of their arguments but in their non-evaluated representation. Although QUOTE has only a single argument, whereas PROGN, IF and DE require at least 0, 2 and 3 respectively, these functions are all said to be of type FSUBR. We will see that in addition to FSUBR we have FEXPR, as well as a fifth class of functions that have not been used up until now, but which are very useful: the macro-functions (of type MEXPR).

All these function types are defined by the functions LAMBDA, NLAMBDA, FLAMBDA and MLAMBDA (these themselves being of type FSUBR).

To summarise, the LISP function is not only defined by a list of variables and a body, but also by its type which indicates the way in which a function is calculated; in other words, it answers the questions:

> Should the arguments be evaluated or not (EVAL/NOEVAL)?
> Should we gather them up with a single list (however many of them there are), or distribute them to the different variables (SPREAD/ NOSPREAD)?
> Finally, what do we do with the value returned after evaluating the function body (MACRO/NOMACRO)?

3.7.2　Environment

The environment, kept by the interpreter, is the data structure which is used to associate each variable with its value. The environment is usually drawn as a sequence of boxes linked together by arrows. Each box contains a group of rows, each of which is made up of an identifier on the left and its associated value on the right. For example, the interpreter's natural environment is as follows:

T	T
NIL	NIL
CAR	*car*
:	:
NULL	⟶ function (LAMBDA (EXP) (EQ EXP NIL))

We will refer to this environment as 'global', so that there will be no need to redraw it later on.

3.7.3 Evaluation of an EXPR form

A form is evaluated in several stages, independently of error recovery.

Let us, for example, evaluate (LE N 1) in the environment:

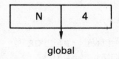

global

Step 1: The first term of the form is evaluated. This must be a function, in which case its type may be deduced. It is an EXPR, so on to Step 2.

Step 2: Successive evaluation of the arguments. In our case, the values of the arguments are 4 and 1 respectively. When all the arguments are evaluated, go on to Step 3.

Step 3: Linking of variables and arguments. Remember that LE is defined as:

   (DE LE (P N)
       (NOT (GT P N)))

A new environment is created, and is shown below:

P	4
N	1

N	4

global

Step 4: The function body is evaluated in this new environment, that is

   (NOT (GT P N))

The value of an identifier in any environment is the one that is stored in the right-hand side of the first row containing the name of this identifier. So, in this case, the value of P is 4 and the value of N is 1 (thus hiding the former value N = 4).

Step 5: When the value of the function (in this case, NIL) is returned on exit, the original environment is restored, in other words, the evaluation continues with

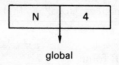

global

and there will be no trace of the former environment. For example, if we enter the following program

```
?(DE FACT (N)
?   (IF (LE N 1)
?       (PROGN (PRINT 'FACTOR:)
?              (EVAL (READ)) )
?       (* N (FACT (SUB1 N))) ) )
    FACT

?(FACT 4)
FACTOR:
?
```

when (READ) is executed, the environment will be

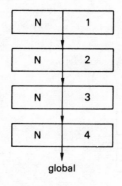

global

as (FACT 4) calls (FACT 3) which calls (FACT 2) which calls (FACT 1)

We may therefore reply

```
?
?(* N N)
    24
```

The answer is 24 as the value of N was 1 in the environment in which the atom FACTOR: was printed.

We will see how the corresponding forms are evaluated for NEXPR, FEXPR, and MEXPR.

■ (LAMBDA (*variables*. . .) *expressions*. . .)

Arguments: *variables*. . . is a possibly empty sequence of identifiers.
expressions is a sequence of any expressions, of which there must be at least one.

Value: A function of type EXPR that has *variables*. . . as a list of variables and *expressions* as a body. Since this function is anonymous (it has not got a name), it is only useful when used as an argument (which will assign a local name to the function) or as the first term of a form.

Applying a LAMBDA-function to its arguments

((LAMBDA (*var1 var2*. . .) *body*. . .)*arg1 arg2*. . .)

means evaluating the *body* assuming that (or in the 'environment' where)

$var1$ = value(*arg1*)
$var2$ = value(*arg2*)
. . .

Example 1

```
?((LAMBDA(X)(PRINT X)) 'EXAMPLE)
EXAMPLE
    EXAMPLE
```

The function, which is the value of the expression (LAMBDA (X) (PRINT X)), is the EXPR equivalent of the function *print*, which is of type SUBR.

But although they have the same value and effect, we find

```
?(EQ PRINT (LAMBDA(X)(PRINT X)))
    NIL
```

as the functions are not of the same type.

Example 2

Suppose that we have a list of numbers (1 2 3 4 5 6) and that we want the list of the cubes of these numbers. We write

```
?(MAPCAR '(1 2 3 4 5 6)
?         (LAMBDA(I)(* I I I)) )
    (1 8 27 64 125 216)
```

The function *cube*, which is the value of the form (LAMBDA (I) (∗ I I I)), is coded anonymously so that it may be forgotten once the evaluation is complete.

MAPCAR is a standard, recursive function which is defined as

```
?(DE MAPCAR (L FN)
?    (IF (CONSP L)
?        (CONS (FN (CAR L))
?              (MAPCAR (CDR L) FN) ) ) )
    MAPCAR
```

The value of MAPCAR is the list that is obtained from the list of the first argument, where the function of the second argument has been applied to each term. This function must of course be monadic, in other words, it must require only a single argument. MAPCAR is one of these functions that you find in any LISP interpreter, but nevertheless, as you may realise, its absence may easily be remedied.

Example 3

This example shows how to create an anonymous function:

```
?(PROGN (DE APPLY ()
?            ((LAMBDA(FN ARG)
?              (PRINT (CONS 'VALUE
?                  (CONS (FN ARG) ; APPLY FN TO ARG
?                      NIL ) ))
?            'END )
?          (PROGN (PRINT 'EXPRESSION-IN-X:)
?              (EVAL (CONS 'LAMBDA ; CREATE A FUNCTION
?                  (CONS '(X)        ; CALCULATING THE
?                                    ; EXPRESSION
?                  (CONS (BASIC-TO-LISP (READ))
?                      NIL ) )))
?          (PROGN (PRINT 'VALUE-OF-X:)
?              (EVAL (READ)) ) ) )
?  (APPLY))
EXPRESSION-IN-X:
?(X ∗ (X + 1) / 2)
VALUE-OF-X:
?(FACT 4)
(VALUE 288)
    END
```

During this evaluation, the value of FN was found to be the function value of (LAMBDA (X) (∗ X (/ (+ X 1) 2)))

Note

The unusual syntax (LAMBDA (*variables*. . .) *expressions*. . .) comes from the
notations associated with Church's λ-calculus (see the entry under A. Church in
the Bibliography in chapter 14).

■ (NLAMBDA (*variable*) *expressions*. . .)

Arguments: *variable* is an identifier. *expressions*. . . is a sequence of any
              expressions, of which there must be at least one.
Value: A function of type NEXPR, which has *variable* as a variable and
             expressions. . . as the body. The created function is anonymous
             and allows any number of arguments. All its arguments are
             evaluated and joined together in a single list which will become
             the value of the identifier *variable*.

Example

```
?((NLAMBDA(L)L) 'MAKES 'A 'LIST)
   (MAKES A LIST)

?((NLAMBDA(L)L)
?  ((NLAMBDA(L)L) 'OF 'ANY 'NUMBER 'OF
?        'EXPRESSIONS ) )
   ((OF ANY NUMBER OF EXPRESSIONS))
```

This function is so useful that it is not kept anonymous. It is called LIST.
    In the same way as DE defines functions of type EXPR, DN will define
functions of type NEXPR. Therefore, if we do not already have it, we write

```
?(DN LIST (L)
?  L )
   LIST

?(LIST 'LIST 'NOT (LIST))
   (LIST NOT NIL)
```

Notes

When the value of the functional term is a function of type NEXPR, the method
for evaluating an EXPR form is altered only in step 3 where the single function
variable is linked to the list of the values of the calling arguments.
    Certain interpreters mix EXPR and NEXPR together by using a cunning
representation of the list of variables. If the latter is an identifier other than
NIL, then the function is an NEXPR, otherwise it is a normal EXPR. For these
interpreters we write

```
?(DE LIST L
?   L )
    LIST

?((LAMBDA L L) 'SAME 'AS 'LIST)
  (SAME AS LIST)
```

This may even allow the simple creation (using dotted pairs) of functions having, at least, a certain number of arguments. For example

```
?((LAMBDA(N1 N2 . N3)
?       (PRINT (LIST 'N1 '= N1))
?       (PRINT (LIST 'N2 '= N2))
?       (PRINT (LIST 'N3 '= N3))
?       T )
? '(A) 'B 'C (LIST) )
(N1 := (A))
(N2 = B)
(N3 := (C NIL))
    T
```

■ (FLAMBDA (*variable*) *expressions*. . .)

Arguments: *variable* is an identifier. *expressions*. . . is a sequence of any
             expressions, of which there must be at least one.
Value: A function of type FEXPR, which has *variable* as a variable and
             expressions. . . as a body. The created function is anonymous. It
             allows any number of arguments. Its arguments are not evaluated
             but are gathered together in a single list which will become the
             value of the identifier *variable*.

Example

```
?((FLAMBDA (ARGS)
?       (PRINT (LIST 'ARGS '= ARGS))
?       T )
? ARG1 ARG2 'ARG3 )
(ARGS = (ARG1 ARG2 (QUOTE ARG3)))
    T
```

Notes
The way to evaluate an FEXPR form is as follows. Let us evaluate

((FLAMBDA (ARGS) (PRINT (LIST 'ARGS '= ARGS))) T)
      ARG1   ARG2   'ARG3)

in the global environment.

Step 1 is common to the evaluation of all forms and involves evaluating the first term of the form in order to find out the function type. Here it is an FEXPR.

Step 2: Linking the single variable (in this case ARGS) to the arguments of the calling form, the following environment is created:

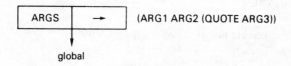

Step 3: Evaluation of the function body in this environment. The form

(PROGN (PRINT (LIST 'ARGS '= ARGS)) T)

will print the list

(ARGS = (ARG1 ARG2 (QUOTE ARG3)))

and will have the value T.

Step 4: The value of the main part is returned and the evaluation continues in the original environment (in this case, the global environment).

FLAMBDA is a function-building facility that is hardly ever used in comparison to LAMBDA or NLAMBDA (we have mentioned it here for the sake of completeness), since there is no great need for an anonymous function of type FEXPR.

As well as having DE and DN, we have DF which enables functions of type FEXPR to be defined. Among other things, functions of type FEXPR allow you to create new control structures: for example, the construction DO *expressions. . .* WHILE *condition*, which enables the execution of *expressions. . .*, then *expressions. . .*, then *expressions. . .* etc. for as long as *condition* remains true. We write

```
?(DF WHILE (ARGS)
?   (WHILE1 (CAR ARGS) (CDR ARGS)) )
    WHILE

?(DE WHILE1 (CONDITION EXPRESSIONS)
?   (IF (EVAL CONDITION)
?       (PROGN (EVAL (CONS 'PROGN
?                          EXPRESSIONS ))
?              (WHILE1 CONDITION
?                      EXPRESSIONS ) ) ) )
    WHILE1
```

The forms present in *expressions. . .* will be evaluated for as long as the value of *condition* is non-NIL. *Condition* is evaluated at the top of the loop whose value will always be NIL.

By using WHILE, we could, for example, rewrite the basic function

```
?(DE TOPLEVEL ()
?   (WHILE T
?           (PRINT (EVAL (READ))) ) )
    TOPLEVEL
```

But FEXPR functions are not used just for that. Consider

```
?(DF QUOTE (ARGS)
?   (CAR ARGS) )
    QUOTE
```

QUOTE is not a primitive function since DF allows you to define QUOTE.

One of the attractions of LISP is that there may be many ways of programming the same object: reconsider the function LIST, which was defined not so long ago as an NEXPR:

```
?(DF LIST (ARGS)
?   (EVAL (LIST1 ARGS)) )
    LIST

?(DE LIST1 (ARGS)
?   (IF ARGS
?        (CONS 'CONS
?               (CONS (CAR ARGS)
?                     (CONS (LIST1 (CDR ARGS))
?                           NIL ) ) ) ) )
    LIST1
```

The value returned by LIST1 is none other than the program that must be evaluated in order to obtain the result. This programming method uses the following relations:

(LIST) may be replaced by NIL
(LIST *expression 1 other expressions*. . .) may be replaced by
(CONS *expression 1* (LIST *other expressions*. . .))

One of LISP's characteristics that should be appreciated is that occasionally it is simpler to calculate the program (the form) whose value is the required result rather than directly to calculate this value.

Notes
In LISP jargon, we say that functions of type

EXPR   are of type EVAL,   SPREAD
NEXPR are of type EVAL,   NOSPREAD
FEXPR are of type NOEVAL, NOSPREAD

EVAL/NOEVAL indicates whether the arguments are evaluated or not, and

SPREAD/NOSPREAD whether the arguments are distributed among the different variables or not.

You will note that NOEVAL, SPREAD functions have not been defined here. They are not generally available, but may easily be written using the FEXPR as a starting point.

- (MLAMBDA (*variable*) *expressions*. . .)

Arguments: *variable* is an identifier and *expressions* is a sequence of any expressions, of which there must be at least one.

Value: A function of type MEXPR (a macro-function) that has a variable called *variable* and *expressions*. . . as its main part. The created function is anonymous. It allows any number of arguments which are not evaluated but the value of *variable* will be the calling form.

A form whose functional term is a macro-function is linked to *variable*. Its body is evaluated and its value replaces the original form ('expansion' stage of the macro-function). This new form is then evaluated instead of the original form, as if the latter had never existed.

Notes

MLAMBDA is a function-building facility which is hardly ever used. As with FLAMBDA, we have mentioned it for the sake of completeness. MEXPR functions are usually defined by the operator DM. Macro-functions can quite conveniently replace FEXPR functions. We can, for example, once again redefine the function LIST:

```
?(DM LIST (CALL)
?   (IF (CDR CALL)
?        (CONS 'CONS
?              (CONS (CADR CALL)
?                    (CONS (CONS 'LIST
?                                (CDDR CALL) )
?                          NIL ) ) )
?        NIL ) )
    LIST
```

You will have noticed that two functions were required when programming LISP as an FEXPR:

LIST whose only aim is to gather up all its arguments into a single list and to give them to
LIST1 which builds the equivalent program

The previous programming method combines these two functions into one and removes the unpleasant result that could arise if we were to write (using the FEXPR definition of LIST)

```
?((NLAMBDA (ARGS) (LIST (CAR ARGS)
?                          (CDR ARGS) ))
? 'ANY 'LIST 'AT-ALL )
  ((CAR ARGS) ((CDR ARGS)))
```

There has obviously been a mistake over the value of ARGS to be used, since we wanted the list (ANY (LIST AT-ALL))! This error (which arises as a result of a conflict over the effect of the normally silent variable, ARGS, which is used in two different contexts) may be partially corrected in an inelegant way if we remove the conflict by using the following FEXPR definition of LIST:

```
? (DF LIST (THIS-VARIABLE-IS-ONLY-USED-BY-LIST)
?    (EVAL (LIST1 THIS-VARIABLE-IS-ONLY-USED-BY-LIST)) )
  LIST
```

This error is, however, completely removed by programming LIST as a macro-function. The explanation for this is as follows.

A form comprising a macro-function will be evaluated by calculating (LIST 'A) in the environment:

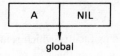

Step 1: Evaluation of the first term of the form; it is a macro-function.

Step 2: Linking the variable with the entire calling form, not just with the list of unevaluated arguments. A new environment is created:

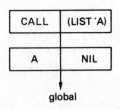

Step 3: The function body is evaluated in this new environment; that is

```
(IF (CDR CALL) (CONS 'CONS (CONS (CADR CALL)
                (CONS (CONS 'LIST (CDDR CALL)) NIL))) NIL)
```

Step 4: After calculation, the value of the function's body is

```
(CONS 'A(LIST))
```

Step 5: Evaluation of this form in the former environment; in other words, evaluation of (CONS 'A (LIST)) with

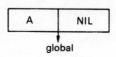

The macro-function calculates an equivalent form which is evaluated on return so as to determine the value of the original form. Later on (see chapter 8), when we talk about destructive macro-functions, we will see the advantage in passing the calling form as an argument and not just the argument list (as with the FEXPR).

Example

The loop DO *expressions*. . . WHILE *condition* which was coded above as an FEXPR, could be better written as a macro-function. Let us give, as an example, the way of programming the loop REPEAT *expressions*. . . UNTIL *condition* which involves evaluating *expressions*. . . for as long as *condition* is false.

```
?(DM UNTIL (CALL)
?    (CONS (LIST 'LAMBDA
?                NIL
?                (LIST 'IF
?                      (CADR CALL) NIL
?                      CALL ) )
?          (CDDR CALL) ) )
     UNTIL
```

We will use this function by writing (UNTIL *condition expressions*. . .)

Example

```
?(DE SKIP (KEY) ; read and skip expressions
?    (UNTIL (EQ (READ) KEY)
?           (PRINT 'SKIP) )
?    'END-OF-SKIP )
     SKIP

?(SKIP 'PLEASE-STOP)
SKIP
?IGNORED
SKIP
?ATOMS
SKIP
?(LIST ALSO)
SKIP
?PLEASE-STOP
     END-OF-SKIP
```

The call to UNTIL generates the expression:

> ((LAMBDA () (IF *condition*
> NIL
> (UNTIL *condition expressions*. . .)
> *expressions*. . .)

You will notice that for the loop REPEAT. . .UNTIL. . ., the test is carried out at the end of the loop, the final value is NIL and we have used the following convenient, standard convention: when a function of type EXPR has more arguments than it needs, these are evaluated but ignored. Thus we have

```
?(PRINT 'ARGUMENT (READ) (PRINT 'NIL))
?T
NIL
ARGUMENT
    ARGUMENT
```

By using this convention, we can redefine PROG1 (see exercise 3.2.4) as

```
?(DE PROG1 (X)
?   X )
    PROG1
```

- (FUNCTIONP *expression*)

Argument: *expression* may have any value.
Value: FUNCTIONP is a predicate that returns T or NIL according to whether the value of *expression* is a function or not.

Four types of function have been analysed. Some interpreters offer others, which may complete those that have been discussed here (for example NOEVAL, SPREAD or MACRO, SPREAD) or which may be totally new (FUNCTION, CLOSURE. . .), but this is beyond the scope of this book.

- Four definition operators correspond to these four function types: DE, DN, DF and DM. These operators are not primitive since they may be programmed in the following manner:

```
?(PROGN (SET 'DF (FLAMBDA (ARGS)
?               (SET (CAR ARGS)
?                   (EVAL (CONS 'FLAMBDA (CDR ARGS)))) )
?               (CAR ARGS) ))
?       ; since df exists, use it
?       (DF DE (ARGS)
?           (SET (CAR ARGS)
?                   (EVAL (CONS 'LAMBDA (CDR ARGS))) )
?           (CAR ARGS) )
```

```
?          (DF DN (ARGS)
?            (SET (CAR ARGS)
?                  (EVAL (CONS 'NLAMBDA (CDR ARGS))) )
?            (CAR ARGS) )
?          (DF DM (ARGS)
?            (SET (CAR ARGS)
?                  (EVAL (CONS 'MLAMBDA (CDR ARGS))) )
?            (CAR ARGS) ) )
      DM
```

This shows that at least SET, LAMBDA, FLAMBDA, NLAMBDA and MLAMBDA are primitive, even though we can write

```
?(DM NLAMBDA (CALL)
?    (LIST 'MLAMBDA
?          '(CALL)
?          (LIST 'LIST
?                (CONS 'LAMBDA
?                       (CDR CALL) )
?                 '(CONS 'LIST
?                        (CDR CALL) ) ) ) )
    NLAMBDA
```

In fact, missing NLAMBDA means that each time we need to evaluate

((NLAMBDA (*variable*) *body*. . .) *arguments*. . .)

we really need to evaluate

((LAMBDA (*variable*) *body*. . .) (LIST *arguments*. . .))

This is what is done in the programming of NLAMBDA. Notice, once again that LISP is made up of a basic core that is ridiculously small when you consider all the interesting programming that can be done, but which is extremely productive considering the power of the functions that can be created (functions with an indefinite number of arguments, your own control structures, etc).

Now only one more function remains to be discussed: the assignment. This function is presented last of all since it is by far the most controversial operator in the whole of LISP. It may seem trivial to write, as in BASIC

LET X = 3

that is, (SET 'X 3) in correct LISP. The exact meaning of this form may differ. We will not describe nor even mention the various assignment methods used by different interpreters (this would need another book), but we will limit ourselves to defining what SET means in this book.

■ (SET *identifier expression*)

Arguments: The value of *identifier* is an identifier. *expression* may have any value.

Value: That of *expression*.
              SET assigns the value of *expression* to the identifier (value of
              identifier).

Example

Consider the following environment:

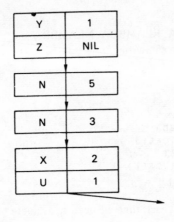

(SET 'X 3) will change the environment to

The form

```
( PROGN ( SET 'Y ( ADD1  X ) )
        ( SET 'CAR CDR )
        ( SET 'N Y )  )
```

changes the environment to

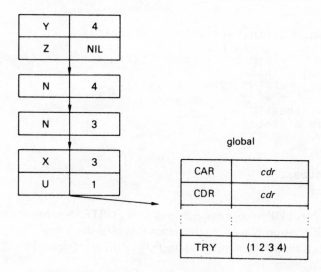

Finally, supposing that the identifier TEST does not appear anywhere in the environment, the form (SET 'TEST (∗ N N)) will change the environment to

In other words, the assignment of a variable means changing the first line where it appears in the current environment. If the variable is not defined in the environment, it is added to the global environment: it will therefore be available to the entire interpreter and will remain there. If you want an assignment to be only temporary, you must make sure that the identifier concerned appears in a list of variables of some function that will cause the assignment to disappear when it returns a value. Consider

```
?(PROGN  ((LAMBDA(Y)(SET 'X 'GLOBAL))
?           'LOCAL )
?         ((LAMBDA(X)(PRINT (LIST 'X 'IS X)))
?           'LOCAL )
?         (PRINT (LIST 'X 'IS X))
?          T )
(X IS LOCAL)
(X IS GLOBAL)
    T

?X
    GLOBAL
```

SET enables LISP to cope perfectly well with FORTRAN programming methods. SET is usually used in interpreters that offer the archaic form PROG, which allows you to program the FORTRAN way (especially with its GOTO statements).

Consider the FORTRAN program

```
        INTEGER FUNCTION PGCD (NX, NY)
100  PGCD = NY
        NZ = MOD (NX,NY)
        IF (NZ. EQ. 0) RETURN
        NX = NY
        NY = NZ
        GOTO 100
        END
```

and the LISP function that calculates the same PGCD

```
?(DE PGCD (NX NY)
?   ((LAMBDA (NZ PGCD) (PGCD1))
?    0 0 ) )
 PGCD

?(DE PGCD1 ()
?   (SET 'PGCD NY)
?   (SET 'NZ (MOD NX NY))
?   (IF (ZEROP NZ)
```

```
?    PGCD
?    (SET 'NX NY)
?    (SET 'NY NZ)
?    (PGCD1) ) )
   PGCD1
```

The function PGCD1 codes the loop with label 100. This programming method is of use only when trying to imitate the FORTRAN model as closely as possible. In fact, it is not far short of resembling its model, but is far from possessing the elegance of the following definition:

```
?(DE PGCD (NX NY)
?    (IF (ZEROP (MOD NX NY))
?       NY
?       (PGCD NY (MOD NX NY)) ) )
   PGCD
```

The previous example, which served to underline the elegance of a recursive definition of PGCD compared to a linear and iterative one, does however have one potentially serious drawback: the expression (MOD NX NY) is calculated twice! If this expression involved a long and costly evaluation (in terms of time and space), then it would be ridiculous to evaluate it twice. The solution involves 'factorisation', where (MOD NX NY) will be calculated once and only once, its value being linked to a local variable NZ, which will itself be used twice. This is a suitable solution since it is easier for the interpreter to determine the value of an identifier than to evaluate some form.

We therefore write

```
?(DE PGCD (NX NY)
?    (LET ((NZ (MOD NX NY)))
?        (IF (ZEROP NZ)
?            NY
?            (PGCD NY NZ) ) ) )
```

The (MOD NX NY) calculation is executed only once and assigned to the local variable NZ, which will disappear once PGCD has been calculated. The form (LET *bindings expressions*. . .) allows the evaluation of *expressions*. . . using local variables which appear in *bindings*. LET is a macro-function replacing

```
(LET ((identifier 1 expression 1)
      (identifier 2 expression 2)
      . . .
      (identifier n expression n) )
      expressions. . .)
```

by

```
((LAMBDA (identifier 1 identifier 2. . . identifier n)
                expressions. . .)
expression 1
expression 2
. . .
expression n)
```

The macro-function LET is defined as follows:

```
?(DM LET (CALL)
?    (CONS (CONS 'LAMBDA
?                 (CONS (MAPCAR (CADR CALL)
?                               CAR )
?                        (CDDR CALL) ) )
?           (MAPCAR (CADR CALL) CADR) ) )
     LET
```

Notice that LET is simultaneous in the sense that its different local variables are all assigned values in parallel. If you wanted to exchange the values of A and B in a certain environment, then you would write

```
(LET ((A B )
      (B A) )...)
```

Example

```
?(PROGN (SET 'A -1)
?       ((LAMBDA(A B)
?           (PRINT (LIST A B))
?           (LET ((A B)
?                 (B A) )
?                (PRINT (LIST A B)) ) )
?         (ADD1 A)
?         (ZEROP A) ) )
(0 NIL)
(NIL 0)
    (NIL 0)
```

On other occasions, you may prefer to assign the values sequentially. For example, if we wished to calculate the first N terms of the Fibonacci series which is defined as

$$U_n = U_{n-1} + U_{n-2}$$

and

$$U_0 = 0, U_1 = 1$$

we would write

```
?(DE FIB (N)
?   (IF (LE N 1) '(1 0)
?        (LETS ((L (FIB (SUB1 N)))
?               (UN-1 (CAR L))
?               (UN-2 (CADR L)) )
?           (CONS (+ UN-1 UN-2) L) ) ) )
    FIB

?(FIB 10)
    ( 55 34 21 13 8 5 3 2 1 1 0)
```

with the macro-function LETS being defined as follows:

```
?(DM LETS (CALL)
?   (IF (CONSP (CADR CALL))
?       (LIST (LIST 'LAMBDA
?                   (LIST (CAAADR CALL))
?                   (CONS 'LETS
?                         (CONS (CDADR CALL)
?                               (CDDR CALL) ) ) )
?             (CADAADR CALL) )
?       (CONS 'PROGN (CDDR CALL)) ) )
    LETS
```

In other words, LETS changes

       (LETS ((*identifier1 expression1*)
            (*identifier2 expression 2*)

            . . .

            (*identifier n expression n*))
            expressions. . .)

into

      ((LAMBDA (*identifier1*)
        ((LAMBDA (*identifier2*)

          . . .

            ((LAMBDA (*identifier n*)
              (PROGN *expressions*. . .))
            expression n)

         . . .

       expression2)
     expression1)

LET and LETS are useful macro-functions which are standard in good interpreters. They may be compared with the BEGIN. . .END blocks of certain languages (ALGOL 60, 68, etc.) where local variables may be declared.

3.7.4 Conclusions

The micro-manual is now complete. We have discussed most of the primitive functions in LISP and some of the more common functions. We have purposely not exhausted the subject area because, firstly, this would require a much larger and more detailed book and, secondly, the analysis of all the different functions and the main characteristics that they have on different interpreters would prove to be quite tedious. Equipped with this basic knowledge of LISP, we will now start to tackle the second part of this book: how to program in LISP, with style.

3.8 Exercises

3.8.1 Write the function WHILE (given in the text as an FEXPR) as a macro-function.
Compare the two programming methods by using

```
(LET ((CONDITION (EVAL (READ))))
     (WHILE CONDITION
            (PRINT 'AGAIN) ) )
```

3.8.2 Write FLAMBDA using only LAMBDA and MLAMBDA.

3.8.3 Write a function that gives the signature of its argument. For example

> (SIGNATURE 31) has the value NUMBERP
> (SIGNATURE '(A(31))) has the value (IDP (NUMBERP))

and

> (SIGNATURE (CONS CAR (CONS (ADD1 0) NIL))) has the value
> (FUNCTIONP NUMBERP)

3.8.4 Write a predicate that has as arguments a signature and an expression and which returns T if the signature of the expression equals the first argument signature.

3.8.5 Write a predicate for list equality. For example

```
?(EQUAL '(A (B) ((C) D))
?         '(A (B) ((C) D)) )
   T
```

PART TWO
PROGRAMMING (WELL) IN LISP

In this part of the book we will present some of the various programming techniques encouraged by LISP. Each chapter that follows will be devoted to a particular style and will be illustrated by at least two examples, one of which will always be the same, thus enabling the different styles to be compared. The function used for this example is the function FLAT which we will define informally in the following way.

FLAT takes a list as its argument and the value returned is the list of atoms that make up this original list. Atoms may appear several times if the initial list has several occurrences of them. The function FLAT takes its name from the fact that it removes the internal brackets of the argument list; basically it 'flattens' the list. For example

```
?(FLAT '(A ((B) A) B))
 (A B A B)
```

4 Unsophisticated Style

This style has been called 'unsophisticated' as it is certainly the most generally used and the most lacking in characteristics that have given rise to the names of other styles. In this chapter we will try to give an idea of the techniques used to handle recursion by explaining the main points that comprise the writing of a function.

Consider the programming of the function REVERSE, which returns, as value, its argument list in reverse. Thus

```
?(REVERSE '(A))
  (A)

?(REVERSE '(A B C))
  (C B A)

?(REVERSE '((A)(B C)(D E F)))
  ((D E F) (B C) (A))
```

We shall show how we can solve this problem in LISP, which is a recursive language; in other words, it is a language that allows recursive functions to be defined.

To solve a problem recursively is to deal with a problem in such a way that

either (1) we can rewrite it as one or several simpler problems of the same type, or (2) we know how to solve it quite simply (using 'the test for end of recursion' or the 'trivial case').

To return a list, the trivial case is when the empty list is obtained after reversing the empty list. In the case where the list is not empty, we can diagrammatically represent this list, as well as the result obtained, by

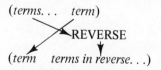

If we assume that we have a function called LAST that gives the last term of a list, as well as the complementary function ALL-BUT-LAST, then we may write

```
(DE REVERSE (L)
   (IF (CONSP L)       ; if not empty
       (CONS (LAST L)
             (REVERSE (ALL-BUT-LAST L)) ) ) )
```

The function LAST will be defined recursively in the following way. If the list has only a single term, then this term is the result:

(*result*)

If it has several terms, we will represent this as

(*term terms*. . .)

As *term* cannot be the last term of this list, we must look for this last term in the new list (*terms*. . .).
We therefore write

```
(DE LAST (L)
   (IF (CONSP (CDR L))
       (LAST (CDR L))      ; search again
       (CAR L) ) )
```

The complementary function ALL-BUT-LAST, which gives a list without its last term, may be written in a similar manner:

```
(DE ALL-BUT-LAST (L)
   (IF (CONSP (CDR L))
       (CONS (CAR L)
             (ALL-BUT-LAST (CDR L)) ) ) )
```

The main problem when programming (recursively or not) is to find the relation that enables the problem to be solved. Relations may not necessarily be usable and may not necessarily lead to comparable programming methods. As an example, the programming method for REVERSE, which is suggested above, is not the one that is usually found in LISP interpreters (as it is not quick enough). The preferred method shown below is based on the other relation:

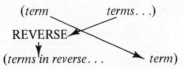

which corresponds (although NCONC (see chapter 8) would, in this case, be a more efficient substitute for APPEND) to

```
(DE REVERSE (L)
  (IF (CONSP L)
      (APPEND (REVERSE (CDR L))
              (LIST (CAR L)) ) ) )
```

The function APPEND enables lists to be concatenated; for example

```
?(APPEND '(A (B)) '((C) D))
  (A (B) (C) D)
```

Of course, APPEND is programmed recursively:

```
(DE APPEND (L1 L2)
  (IF (CONSP L1)

      (CONS (CAR L1)
            (APPEND (CDR L1) L2) )
      L2 ) )
```

The functions APPEND and REVERSE are found in any interpreter worth the name.

■ FLAT

Let us look more closely at a problem that has been briefly introduced. The argument required by FLAT may be any expression; if it is an atom, we will return a list comprising this single atom. Thus

```
?(FLAT 'ATOM)
  (ATOM)
```

On the other hand, if this atom is NIL, we will disregard it. This decision has been taken because we have said that we wish to remove internal brackets, so (FLAT '(ATOM NIL)) should be treated as

(FLAT '(ATOM ()))

whose value will be (ATOM).

First solution
If the argument is a non-empty list, then we can distinguish between two situations, one where the first term is a non-empty list and the other where it is not.

((*terms. . .*)   *other terms. . .*)
    ↓   ↓
  FLAT   FLAT
    ↓   ↓
(*flattened terms. . .*   *other flattened terms. . .*)

or

(*atom*   *other terms. . .*)
 | FLAT
 | ↓
 ↓
(*atom*   *other flattened terms. . .*)

We therefore know enough to be able to write

```
(DE FLAT (L)
  (IF (ATOM L)
       (IF (NULL L)       ; ignore nil
           NIL
           (LIST L) )
       (IF (ATOM (CAR L))     ; recurse
           (CONS (CAR L)(FLAT (CDR L)))
           (APPEND (FLAT (CAR L))
                   (FLAT (CDR L)) ) ) ) )
```

This is a rough program which has a lot of potential. Firstly, we can rewrite
(IF (NULL L) NIL (LIST L)) as

    (IF L (LIST L))

Then we can note that there are two tests for atomic values (use of the predicate
ATOM). We also have the equality

    (APPEND (LIST (CAR L)) (FLAT (CDR L)))
    =(CONS (CAR L) (FLAT (CDR L)))

(To prove this equality you just need to return to the definition of APPEND or
use a theorem prover (written in LISP of course) which will easily be able to
establish this equality.)
All these simplifications lead to

```
(DE FLAT (L)
  (IF (ATOM L)
       (IF L (LIST L))
       (APPEND (FLAT (CAR L))
               (FLAT (CDR L)) ) ) )
```

Second solution
The previous solution was based on the fact that we were treating lists as being

    (*first term   other terms. . .*)

which is useful since this structure results from consideration of the CAR and CDR facilities. We will develop another solution for FLAT, where a list is considered as comprising a list of terms; the solution plan will be

$$(term\ 1 \qquad term\ 2 \qquad \dots\ term\ n)$$
$$\downarrow \qquad\qquad \downarrow \qquad\qquad\quad \downarrow$$
$$FLAT \qquad FLAT \qquad \dots\ FLAT$$
$$\downarrow \qquad\qquad \downarrow \qquad\qquad\quad \downarrow$$
$$(term\ 1\ flattened \quad term\ 2\ flattened\ \dots\ term\ n\ flattened)$$

All we need write therefore is

```
(DE FLAT (L)
   (IF (ATOM L)
       (IF L (LIST L))
       (MAPCAN (MAPCAR L FLAT)
               (LAMBDA(X) X) ) ) )
```

We have already come across the recursive function MAPCAR (see LAMBDA in chapter 3). MAPCAN is another recursive function which is only slightly different (CONS is replaced by APPEND).

```
(DE MAPCAN (L FN)
   (IF (CONSP L)
       (APPEND (FN (CAR L))
               (MAPCAN (CDR L) FN) ) ) )
```

Therefore, if FLAT's argument is a non-empty list, we apply FLAT to each term of the list (these calculations could even be applied in parallel) and we get a list where each term is the flattened version of the corresponding term. All we need do is carry out a generalised APPEND (by MAPCAN) on this list to get the result.

These two solutions show two important points:

(1) Before looking for any improvements, it is important to have a correct program (even if it is clumsy). Once you have this reference point, you can then improve, rewrite, compare, etc.
(2) When you have a function to write, you must find a relation in order to be able to program the function: it often pays to follow the syntax structure.

4.1 Exercises

4.1.1 Write the function MIRROR that gives the complete mirror image of its argument. Thus

```
?(MIRROR '((A B)((C D) E)))
  ((E (D C)) (B A))
```

4.1.2 Write a function EGYPT which, for a fraction p/q calculates a list of Egyptian fractions whose sum is equal to p/q. Remember that the numerator of an Egyptian fraction is 1. For example

```
?(EGYPT 3 4)
  (2 4)
```

which is obtained by saying

$$\frac{3}{4} = \frac{1}{2} + \frac{1}{4}$$

We apply the following method (from Gauss). Find n such that

$$\frac{1}{n} \leqslant \frac{p}{q} < \frac{1}{n-1}$$

Keep $1/n$ and repeat with the new fraction

$$\frac{p}{q} - \frac{1}{n}$$

4.1.3 Write the predicate MEMBER, which tests whether the first argument atom is, or is not, a term of the second argument list; for example

```
?(MEMBER 'ATOM '(IF (ATOM L) NIL))
  NIL

?(MEMBER 'NIL '(IF (ATOM L) NIL))
  T
```

5 Buffer Variables

Functions that are built in this style have one or several extra arguments which are used to store parts of future results, or data to be handled later on. Here is an example:

```
(DE FLAT (L)
   (FLAT1 L NIL) )
```

FLAT is merely the interface between the user and the function FLAT1 which carries out the flattening process:

```
(DE FLAT1 (L RESULT)
   (IF (ATOM L)
       (IF L (CONS L RESULT)
           RESULT )
       (FLAT1 (CAR L)
              (FLAT1 (CDR L)
                     RESULT ) ) ) )
```

FLAT1 uses two variables L and RESULT. L is the expression to be analysed and RESULT is used to store the different atoms (non-NIL) which have already been found. FLAT1 uses an overlapping, double recursive call which consists in calculating the flattened list of the argument list (except its first term), then in using this result when calculating the flattened list of the first term. This final calculation completes the result (from the left) using the atoms already found. If we trace FLAT1 using the following example, we have

```
?(TRACE FLAT1)
   (FLAT1)

?(FLAT '((A B) ((C) D)) NIL))
(FLAT1 ((A B) ((C) D)) NIL)
  (FLAT1 (((C) D)) NIL)
   (FLAT1 NIL NIL)
   NIL
   (FLAT1 ((C) D) NIL)
    (FLAT1 (D) NIL)
     (FLAT1 NIL NIL)
     NIL
```

75

```
        (FLAT1 D NIL)
        (D)
        (D)
      (FLAT1 (C) (D))
        (FLAT1 NIL (D))
        (D)
        (FLAT1 C (D))
        (C D)
        (C D)
      (C D)
    (C D)
    (FLAT1 (A B) (C D))
      (FLAT1 (B) (C D))
        (FLAT1 NIL (C D))
        (C D)
        (FLAT1 B (C D))
        (B C D)
      (B C D)
      (FLAT1 A (B C D))
      (A B C D)
    (A B C D)
  (A B C D)
    (A B C D)
```

This style is similar to the one known as 'continuations', which we will not show here, but which consists in being able to explicitly handle the sequence of remaining calculations in order to get a final value. In our case, a partial result can be handled indefinitely (see exercise 5.1.1).

Generally, functions that use buffer variables simply initialise these variables, and let the sub-functions perform the necessary evaluations. In the situation

$$(FLAT1 \ '((A \ B) \ ((C) \ D)))$$

(this form is incorrect since there is no second argument) certain interpreters generate as many NILS as there are missing arguments, which enables functions to be merged (FLAT1 will disappear here) in the case where the initialisation values are exactly equal to NIL. Other interpreters, when faced with an incorrect form, will link the variables having no argument to a special internal value ('UNDEFINED'). Any attempt to evaluate a variable whose value is undefined would cause an error. The interpreter in this book is of this second sort.

In order to progress from the unsophisticated style to this present style, let us give some indications as to the changes to be undertaken. In the simple definition of FLAT, the value is

(1) either the constant NIL, or
(2) directly built by LIST, or
(3) the result of a concatenation (APPEND).

In brief, the final value is the result of a form containing only APPEND, (LIST *atom*) and NIL. Let us introduce the variable RESULT:

```
(DE FLAT1 (L RESULT)
  (IF (ATOM L)
       (IF L (APPEND (LIST L) RESULT)
            (APPEND NIL RESULT) )
       (APPEND (APPEND (FLAT (CAR L))
                        (FLAT (CDR L)) )
              RESULT ) ) )
```

If you examine the properties of APPEND, you will notice that the following relations can be proved:

(APPEND (LIST L) RESULT) = (CONS L RESULT)
(APPEND NIL RESULT) = RESULT
(APPEND (APPEND *expression 1 expression 2*) *expression 3*) =
(APPEND *expression 1* (APPEND *expression 2 expression 3*))

As an example we shall prove the first equation:

(APPEND (LIST L) RESULT) is equivalent to
(IF (CONSP (LIST L))
    (CONS (CAR (LIST L))
          (APPEND (CDR (LIST L)) RESULT))
    RESULT)

This gives us

(CONS L (APPEND NIL RESULT))

since (CONSP (LIST L)) is always true, and furthermore

(CAR (LIST L)) = (CAR (CONS L NIL)) = L
(CDR (LIST L)) = (CDR (CONS L NIL)) = NIL

Working along the same lines

(APPEND NIL RESULT) = RESULT

which therefore proves the above equation.
Now we can simplify the definition of FLAT1 to

```
(DE FLAT1 (L RESULT)
  (IF (ATOM L)
       (IF L (CONS L RESULT) RESULT)
       (APPEND (FLAT (CAR L))
              (APPEND (FLAT (CDR L))
                       RESULT ) ) ) )
```

We also have

(APPEND (FLAT *expression 1*) *expression 2*) =
(FLAT1 *expression 1 expression 2*)

So we arrive at the final version of FLAT1.

This sort of handling may be carried out automatically by programs (written in LISP) that are used to alter other programs and that are able to apply these alterations correctly, by using a knowledge database (containing, for example the equalities used above).

■ The following example uses this same technique. What we are doing is defining a function that takes a labyrinth as input and that produces the escape path from this labyrinth as its value.

```
?(DE THESEUS (LABYRINTH)
?    (ARIADNE (START LABYRINTH) START-THREAD) )
     THESEUS

?(DE ARIADNE (PLACE THREAD)
?    (COND ((EXIT? PLACE) (UNWIND THREAD PLACE))
?          ((OR (SEEN-BEFORE? PLACE THREAD)
?               (CUL-DE-SAC? PLACE) ) GOBACK)
?          (T (FOR-EVERYONE (NEIGHBOURS PLACE)
?                           (LAMBDA (NEIGHBOUR)
?                           (ARIADNE NEIGHBOUR
?                                 (UNWIND THREAD PLACE)))
?              )) ) )
     ARIADNE
?(DE FOR-EVERYONE (NEIGHBOURHOOD DO)
?    (IF (AGAIN? NEIGHBOURHOOD)
?        (LET ((TRY (DO (FIRST NEIGHBOURHOOD))))
?             (IF TRY TRY
?                 (FOR-EVERYONE (OTHERS NEIGHBOURHOOD) DO)
?        GOBACK ) )
```

Before expanding these definitions, it is appropriate to introduce the standard functions COND and OR.

■ (COND(*predicate 1 expressions 1 . . .*)
        (*predicate 2 expressions 2 . . .*)
         . . .   .
        (*predicate n expressions n . . .*))

COND is defined as follows:

```
(DM COND (CALL)
  (IF (CONSP (CDR CALL))
     (LIST 'IF
        (CAADR CALL)
        (CONS 'PROGN (CDADR CALL))
        (CONS 'COND (CDDR CALL)) ) ) )
```

COND is a conditional expression (like IF), and is often taken as being the basic conditional expression instead of IF (one may be defined from the other and vice versa). A COND form is more legible than the equivalent form:

(IF *predicate 1* (PROGN *expressions 1 . . .*)
  (IF *predicate 2* (PROGN *expressions 2. . .*)

    . . .

      (IF *predicate n* (PROGN *expressions n. . .*)
      NIL). . .))

■ (OR *expression 1 expression 2 . . .expression n*)

The function OR represents the standard Boolean OR and is defined thus:

```
(DM OR (CALL)
  (IF (CONSP (CDR CALL))
     (LIST 'IF (CADR CALL) T
              (CONS 'OR (CDDR CALL)) )
     NIL ) )
```

An OR form generates the equivalent expression:

(IF *expression 1* T (OR *expression 2 . . .expression n*))

The important characteristic of the OR function is that it evaluates its arguments one after another for as long as the value of these arguments is NIL. The first argument whose value is different from NIL interrupts the OR function, which does not evaluate the following arguments but immediately returns the value T. For example

```
?(OR (NULL (CAR '(LIST)))
?    (OR)
?    (CAR '(LIST))
?    (PRINT 'ERROR) )
   T
```

As well as OR, there is a function AND which is defined as

```
?(DM AND (CALL)
?  (IF (CONSP (CDR CALL))
?      (LIST 'IF (CADR CALL)
```

```
?                          (CONS 'AND (CDDR CALL)) )
?         T ) )
     AND

?(AND (AND)
?         (NULL 'LIST)
?         (PRINT 'ERROR) )
     NIL
```

■ The function THESEUS takes a labyrinth as its argument and by calling ARIADNE produces the path leading to the exit. The call to ARIADNE is carried out using the starting place with a thread which is initially empty (the thread is the buffer variable).

The algorithm used to find the way out of the labyrinth is as follows. If you are not at the exit, then you must carry on ahead! If you are neither at a cul-de-sac (in which case you can only go back) nor at a place you have already been through (in which case you are going round in circles and so you must therefore look elsewhere, that is, you must go back) then you must be in a new place and all departing routes will be explored.

So as to make the central algorithm (ARIADNE) more legible and not to complicate it by the special representation of the labyrinth, we have used a large number of new identifiers (START, START-THREAD, etc.) which represent either constants or functions that allow us to extract information about the labyrinth. We can therefore alter the representation of the labyrinth without having to change the central algorithm and vice versa.

We will represent a labyrinth as

((*place of exit 1 . . .place of exit n*)
  (*place 1 places next to 1. . .*)
  (*place 2 places next to 2. . .*)
  . . .   .
  (*place p places next to p. . .*)))

ARIADNE's thread is the collection of successive places through which we have passed (the starting place being the first to appear in this list). The constants and utility functions are therefore

```
?(SET 'GOBACK NIL)
?(SET 'START-THREAD NIL)
?(DE UNWIND (THREAD PLACE)
    (APPEND THREAD (LIST PLACE)) )
```

NEIGHBOURHOOD represents a collection of places which are acted upon by

```
?(SET 'AGAIN? CR)        ; CR IS THE IDENTITY FUNCTION
?(SET 'FIRST CAR)
?(SET 'OTHERS CDR)
```

PLACE is an atom defined in the labyrinth.

```
?(DE EXIT? (PLACE)
?    (MEMBER PLACE (CAR LABYRINTH)) )
?(DE CUL-DE-SAC? (PLACE)
?    (NULL (NEIGHBOURS PLACE)) )
?(DE NEIGHBOURS (PLACE)
?    (CDR (ASSOC PLACE (CDR LABYRINTH))) )
?(DE START (LABYRINTH)
?    (CAADR LABYRINTH) )
?(SET 'SEEN-BEFORE MEMBER)
```

These definitions have introduced us to two new standard functions: MEMBER and ASSOC.

■ (MEMBER *atom list*)

MEMBER is a predicate which tests if an *atom* belongs to a *list* (see exercise 4.1.3). MEMBER is defined as

```
(DE MEMBER (A L)
  (AND (CONSP L)
       (OR (EQ A (CAR L))
           (MEMBER A (CDR L)) ) ) )
```

■ (ASSOC *indicator A-list*)

ASSOC introduces us to the world of 'Association-lists', abbreviated to 'A-lists'. An A-list is a data structure that is used a great deal in LISP (the environments kept by the interpreter are often represented as A-lists). An A-list may be seen as

((*indicator 1 values 1...*) (*indicator 2 values 2...*)...)

indicator is an atom and *values...* is a sequence of any LISP expressions. ASSOC is defined as

```
(DE ASSOC (I AL)
  (IF AL
      (IF (EQ (CAAR AL) I)
          (CAR AL)
          (ASSOC I (CDR AL)) ) ) )
```

ASSOC allows us to search the second argument A-list for a pair (if there is one) whose indicator is *indicator*. The (*indicator values...*) pair is returned, instead of just the associated value, so that we can distinguish between the absence of a pair and an associated NIL value.

The A-list allows us therefore to store *values...* which may be retrieved by associated *indicators*.

All that remains is to confront THESEUS with the following labyrinth:

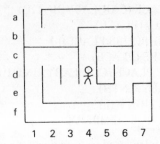

which we will represent as

```
(SET 'LABYRINTH '
((A1)      ; a single exit
 (D4  C4  E4)(B1  A1  B2)(B2  B1  B3  A2)(B3  B2  A3)(A2  B2  A3)
 (A3  A2  B3  A4)(A4  A3  A5)(A5  A4  A6)(A6  A5  A7)(A7  A6  B7)
 (B7  A7  C7)(C7  B7  D7)(D7  C7  D6)(D6  C6  E6)(C6  D6  C5)
 (C5  D5  C6)(E6  D6  E5)(E5  E4  E6)(E4  E5  E3  D4)(A1  B1)
 (C4  B4  D4)(B4  C4  B5)(B5  B4  B6)(B6  B5)(E3  E4  E2  D3)
 (D3  E3  C3)(C3  D3  C2)(C2  C1  C3  D2)(D2  C2  E2)(E2  D2  E3)
 (C1  C2  D1)(D1  C1  E1)(E1  D1  F1)(F1  E1  F2)(F2  F1  F3)
 (F3  F2  F4)(F4  F3  F5)(F5  F4  F6)(F6  F5  F7)(F7  F6  E7)
 (E7  F7)  )  )
```

The way in which ARIADNE is programmed illustrates the use of a 'back tracking' algorithm. If we imagine the variable THREAD each time it is changed (for example, by tracing UNWIND) we get

(D4) ; departure point
(D4 C4)
(D4 C4 B4)
(D4 C4 B4 B5)
(D4 C4 B4 B5 B6) ; failure
(D4 E4) ; return to last crossroads
(D4 E4 E5)
(D4 E4 E5 E6)
(D4 E4 E5 E6 D6)
(D4 E4 E5 E6 D6 C6)
(D4 E4 E5 E6 D6 C6 C5)
(D4 E4 E5 E6 D6 C6 C5 D5) ; failure
(D4 E4 E5 E6 D6 D7) ; return to last crossroads
. . . . . . ; jump a few stages
(D4 E4 E5 E6 D6 D7 C7 B7 A7 A6 A5 A4 A3 A2 B2 B1 A1) ; success!

The labyrinth is explored path by path until we find one that leads to the exit. In the case of failure, we return to the last crossroads where there was an unexplored branch. We admit final defeat (NIL) when the entire labyrinth has been explored in vain.

5.1 Exercises

5.1.1 Write the function ATOMS which, for any expression, gives the list of all the different atoms that make up this expression.

5.1.2 Write a version of factorial using a buffer variable.

5.1.3 Define the conditional expression IF using COND.

5.1.4 Change the function THESEUS and its associates so as to avoid the situation where, if two points a and b are next to each other, we have both

(a ... b ...) and (b ... a ...)

in the list representing the labyrinth.

As the neighbourhood relation is symmetrical (if a is next to b, then b is next to a), it is useless having this duplicate information.

6 Data Driven Programming

This style is one of the most exciting in LISP. Data driven programming is modular and expandable. It is based on the idea of a property list (abbreviated to 'P-list'). Each identifier has an associated P-list. We handle these P-lists by using the functions PUT and GET. P-lists are often (but not always) A-lists which, like the environment, are handled only by the interpreter.

■ (PUT *identifier indicator value*)

Arguments: *identifier* and *indicator* have identifiers as value and any object
may be the value of *value*.

Value: That of *identifier*. PUT places the value (value of *value*) under the
property indicator (value of *indicator*) in the P-list of the atom
(value of *identifier*). You may have as many properties as you wish.

■ (GET *identifier indicator*)

Arguments: The values of *identifier* and *indicator* are identifiers.

Value: If there is an object placed under the property indicator (value of
indicator) in the P-list of the atom (value of *identifier*), then the
value of the GET form will be this object, otherwise the value will
be NIL.

Note

We do not distinguish between the absence of a property and a property whose value is NIL. We can therefore remove a property by evaluating (PUT *identifier indicator* NIL).

Examples

```
?(GET 'JOE 'NATURE)
   NIL

?(PUT 'JOE 'NATURE 'HAPPY)
   JOE

?(GET 'JOE 'NATURE)
   HAPPY

?(PUT 'JOE 'NATURE 'SAD)
   JOE
```

```
?(PUT 'JOJO 'ALIAS 'JOE)
   JOJO

?(GET (GET 'JOJO 'ALIAS) 'NATURE)
   SAD

?(PUT (PUT 'JOE 'ALIAS NIL) 'NATURE NIL)
   JOE

?(GET 'JOE 'NATURE)
   NIL
```

■ You will have noticed in previous chapters, and especially during the discussion of macro-functions, that we kept on building lists where often the variable parts were a small proportion compared to the fixed parts. For example, the aim of the OR definition (see chapter 5) was to build the list

(IF (CADR CALL) T (OR (CDDR CALL)))

The underlined expressions are replaced in two very distinct ways:

(CADR CALL) must be replaced by its value

(CDDR CALL) must be replaced by the terms that make up its value
                        (which must therefore be a list)

For example, if the value of CALL is (OR(OR) (ADD1 A)T), the list to be generated will be

(IF (OR) T (OR (ADD1 A) T))

In order to avoid long and tedious sequences of CONS, LIST and QUOTE (which would make legibility difficult), to generate these expressions we call the function BUILD. We therefore write

```
(DM OR (CALL)
   (IF (CONSP (CDR CALL))
       (BUILD '(IF (:= (CADR CALL))
                   T
                   (OR (:↑ (CDDR CALL))) )) ) )
```

The symbols := and :↑ indicate the places and the substitution modes with which BUILD deals. We write BUILD as

```
(DE BUILD (L)
  (IF (CONSP L)
      (IF (CONSP (CAR L))
          (COND((EQ (CAAR L) ':=)
                (CONS (EVAL (CADAR L))
                      (BUILD (CDR L)) ) )
               ((EQ (CAAR L) ':↑)
                (APPEND (EVAL (CADAR L))
                        (BUILD (CDR L)) ) )
               (T (CONS (BUILD (CAR L))
                        (BUILD (CDR L)) )) ) )
          (CONS (CAR L)(BUILD (CDR L))) )
      L ) )
```

To define BUILD using data driven programming we write

```
(DE BUILD (L)
  (IF (CONSP L)
      (IF (CONSP (CAR L))
          (LET ((FN (GET 'BUILD (CAAR L))))
               (IF FN (FN L)
                      (CONS (BUILD (CAR L))
                            (BUILD (CDR L)) ) ) )
          (CONS (CAR L)(BUILD (CDR L))) )
      L ) )
```

Without forgetting

```
(PUT 'BUILD ':= (LAMBDA(L)              ; cons is used
     (CONS (EVAL (CADAR L))             ; to replace a term
           (BUILD (CDR L)) ) ))         ; by another one


(PUT 'BUILD ':↑ (LAMBDA(L)              ; append is used
     (APPEND (EVAL (CADAR L))           ; to replace a term
             (BUILD (CDR L)) ) ))       ; by a sequence of terms
```

   The differences in the second version compared to the first have been underlined. Any special processing to be done when := or :↑ are encountered is
transferred outside of the central algorithm and dealt with by the functions
placed in the P-list of BUILD. The two programs are equivalent apart from the
introduction of the extra local variable FN. The basic point of data driven
programming is that if you wish to increase the set of existing operators (:= and
:↑), then the first solution means changing the code for the function BUILD,
which may cause errors and may make the entire function illegible, while the
second simply requires a new property on the P-list of BUILD. For example

```
( PUT  'BUILD  ' : *  ( LAMBDA( L )
      ( APPEND  ( EXPAND  ( EVAL  ( CADAR  L ) ) )
                ( BUILD  ( CDR  L ) )  )  ) )
```

with

```
( DE  EXPAND  ( N )     ; the A.P.L. iota function
   ( IF  ( GT  N  0 )
         ( APPEND  ( EXPAND  ( SUB1  N ) )
                   ( LIST  N )  )  )  )
```

We can therefore redefine factorial as

```
( DM  FACT  ( CALL )
   ( LET  ( ( N  ( EVAL  ( CADR  CALL ) ) ) )
          ( BUILD  ' ( TIMES  ( : *  N ) ) )  )  )
```

By doing this, (FACT (ADD1 4)) will generate (TIMES 1 2 3 4 5) whose value is the one required.

With data driven programming, the data are decomposed according to their list structure. Each list undergoes the treatment indicated by the identifier in function position (or a standard treatment if it has no associated property). In the case of BUILD, in order to exploit the difference between CONS and APPEND (required by := and :↑ respectively), we are not interested in the CAR, but in the CAAR of the lists.

Data driven programming is characterised by the form

(DE *function* (*variable*)
  (IF (CONSP *variable*)
    (LET ((FN (GET '*function* (CAR *variable*))))
      (IF FN (FN *variable*)
        standard treatment for list))
      standard treatment for atom))

A variation on this may be to store an expression, and not a function, on the P-list of *function*. Therefore the 3rd and 4th lines are replaced by

(LET ((EXP (GET '*function* (CAR *variable*))))
  (IF EXP (EVAL EXP)

An interesting characteristic of GET is that if the value of its second argument (indicator) is not an identifier, then the value returned by GET is always NIL. This means we can avoid testing the atomicity of the CAR of the list which would otherwise mean having to write something like

(DE *function* (*variable*)
  (IF (CONSP *variable*)

$$(IF (AND (ATOM (CAR \textit{variable}))$$
$$(GET \textit{'function} (CAR \textit{variable})))$$
$$((GET \textit{'function} (CAR \textit{variable})) \textit{variable})$$

standard treatment for list)

standard treatment for atom))

Note

The variation suggested above does not make use of any local variable, but does require two recalculations of the expression (GET *'function* (CAR *variable*)) (when there is a property to bring into play).

You will also note the expression

((GET *'function* (CAR *variable*)) variable)

where the function to be applied is the result of a calculation. This is more complex than in the ordinary situation where the function is simply the value of an atom.

To sum up, data driven programming enables us to have algorithms that are short (the central algorithm has been described above), modular (each particular case is referred to the P-list and is independent of whether others are present or not) and expandable (without changing any properties that already exist, you can add new ones). This rich style may be considered as the ancestor of pattern-matching programming, where it is no longer just the atom in function position that initiates a certain treatment, but the structure of the entire list (compare the function MICRO-MATCH in chapter 10, section 10.3).

FLAT does not immediately lend itself to being written in this style. The following attempt is therefore to be considered simply as a borderline case, which is to be avoided rather than copied since it involves replacing a simple conditional expression (IF (PAIRP L). . .) by a program that is driven by the type of data (and not by the data itself). Notice that here, the standard schema has been modified by using a new conditional function called OR! This conditional function, whose clever coding appears below, returns NIL if the value of all its arguments is NIL, or, if not, returns (not T, but) the value of the first non-NIL argument. (Compare this with the Boolean definition given in chapter 5).

```
?(DM OR (CALL)
?    (IF (CONSP (CDR CALL))
?        (IF (CONSP (CDDR CALL))
?            (BUILD '(EVAL ((LAMBDA (X)
?        (IF X (LIST 'QUOTE X)
?            (CONS 'OR '(:= (CDDR CALL))) ) )
?                              (:= (CADR CALL)) )))
?            (CADR CALL) ) ) )
     OR
?
?(LETS ((Y 3)(X (NOT Y)))
?        (OR X Y (PRINT T)) )
     3
```

As we would expect, there is also a conditional version of the function AND, which returns NIL if the value of one of its arguments is NIL, or otherwise returns the value of its last argument.

```
? ( DM AND ( CALL )
?   ( IF ( CONSP ( CDR CALL ) )
?        ( IF ( CONSP ( CDDR CALL ) )
?             ( LIST 'IF
?                      ( CADR CALL )
?                      ( CONS 'AND ( CDDR CALL ) ) )
?                ( CADR CALL ) )
?        T ) )
   AND
?
? ( AND 1 2 3 )
   3
```

Now that once these definitions have been established, we may write the new version of FLAT:

```
( DE FLAT ( L )
  ( ( OR ( GET 'FLAT ( TYPE L ) )
         ( LAMBDA( L ) ( IF L ( LIST L ) ) ) )
  L ) )


( PUT 'FLAT 'CONSP
   ( LAMBDA( L ) ( MAPCAN ( MAPCAR L FLAT )
                          CR ) ) )
( DE TYPE ( EXP )
   ( COND ( ( CONSP EXP ) 'CONSP )
          ( ( SYMBOLP EXP ) 'SYMBOLP )
          ( ( NUMBERP EXP ) 'NUMBERP )
          ( ( FUNCTIONP EXP ) 'FUNCTIONP ) ) )
```

6.1 Exercises

6.1.1 Write the macro-functions UNTIL and NLAMBDA using BUILD.

6.1.2 Write a function CONSTRUCT that builds the program that needs to be evaluated in order to generate the list described by the argument. You should have

(EVAL (CONSTRUCT *expression*)) = (BUILD *expression*)

7 Instantiations of Schemas

FLAT is one of the many examples of a process that involves scanning an entire expression and performing a certain function on each atom. Rather than programming this scan each time, we can write a single function that carries out this process:

```
(DE SWEEP (TREE BUILD PROCESS)
    (SWEEP1 TREE) )
(DE SWEEP1 (TREE)
    ((NEW-CONSP TREE)
     (BUILD (SWEEP1 (CAR TREE))
            (SWEEP1 (CDR TREE)) )
     (PROCESS TREE) ) )
(DE NEW-CONSP (L)
    (IF (CONSP L)
        (MLAMBDA(CALL) (CADR CALL))
        (MLAMBDA(CALL) (CADDR CALL)) ) )
```

NEW-CONSP is a somewhat peculiar function that we have introduced in order to show all the subtle variations that LISP allows. The value of the expression

((NEW-CONSP *argument*) *expression 1 expression 2*)

is the value of *expression 1* or that of *expression 2* according to whether the value of *argument* is a non-empty list or not. Note that only one of the expressions *expression 1* or *expression 2* is evaluated.

The variables BUILD and PROCESS, which belong to the function SWEEP, are all that you need to specify in order to carry out a particular scan of an expression. PROCESS is applied to each atom in the original expression, and the returned values are formed by BUILD.

Using this schema, we may write FLAT as

```
(DE FLAT (L)
    (SWEEP L APPEND
           (LAMBDA(A)(IF A (LIST A))) ))
```

This definition is practically a reproduction of the simple definition of FLAT (see chapter 4). We say that there has been an instantiation of the schema SWEEP, since in fact, the values of BUILD and PROCESS were fixed in the definition of SWEEP1.

90

Many other functions may be adapted to this schema: we will simply use
SUBST, LENGTH and MIRROR as examples:

```
(DE SUBST (X Y Z)
   (SWEEP Z CONS
               (LAMBDA(A)(IF (EQ A Y) X A)) ) )


(DE LENGTH (L)
   (SWEEP L
          (MLAMBDA(CALL)
                   (LIST 'ADD1 (CADDR CALL)) )
          (LAMBDA(A) 0) ) )

(DE MIRROR (L)
   (SWEEP L
          (LAMBDA(X Y)(APPEND Y (LIST X)))
          CR ) )   ; cr is identity
```

where SUBST and LENGTH are two standard LISP functions. SUBST allows all
the atoms Y in the expression Z to be substituted by the expression X.

LENGTH gives the number of terms in its argument:

```
?(LENGTH NIL)
   0

?(LENGTH '(A (B C)))
   2
```

Finally, the function MIRROR (see exercise 4.1.1) returns a list:

```
?(MIRROR '(A (B C)))
   ((C B) A)
```

As with the functions MAPCAR and MAPCAN, the function SWEEP is a
schema that needs to be instantiated in order to achieve a particular process.
Of course, a schema is of use only when used more than once, in other words,
if it has some universal value. There is one important point to note: there may
be problems in the capture of variables if we use functions, which have free
variables, as arguments to the schema. In a function, a variable is considered
free if it appears in the body of this function without belonging to its list of
variables. For example, in

```
(LAMBDA(X) (OR (EQ X NIL) (EQ X L)))
```

OR, EQ, NIL and L are free variables. Usually this does not matter for OR, EQ and NIL, as they are global variables (recognised everywhere and having a constant value). On the other hand, what is the value of L in this expression? Everything depends on the environment! Without going into the solution to this problem (which requires delicate, precise and clever handling of the environments by using the functions FUNCTION or CLOSURE which we will not discuss here, rich though they are in interesting developments (programming by continuations, suspensions, etc.) generating new and very important efficient and elegant styles), since we would then to a large extent go beyond the aim of this book, which is to provide an introduction to LISP, let us mention that the problem of capturing variables has already been met (when programming WHILE or LIST, see chapter 7) and stems from the collision between free variables and variables of functions of type FEXPR or NEXPR which have similar names. As a precaution, the variables TREE, BUILD and PROCESS are banned as free variables of the function arguments of SWEEP.

7.1   Exercises

7.1.1 Write the functions SUBST and LENGTH in their simple form.

7.1.2 Using the schema SWEEP, write a function that counts the number of non-NIL atoms in an expression.

7.1.3 Define the schema LIT such that

> (LIT '(*term 1 term 2 . . .term n*) '*end* '*function*) generates
> (*function* '*term 1*
>   (*function* '*term 2*
>   . . .   (*function* '*term n* '*end*). . .))

7.1.4 Using LIT, write a function that removes all the occurrences of an atom as a term in a list.

```
?(DELETE 'A '(A B C (A B) C B A))
 (B C (A B) C B)
```

8 Inside LISP

The chapter does not deal with a particular programming style, but provides an interlude, the purpose of which is to introduce two extra primitives as well as to offer a quick look into the organisation of the LISP memory.

We have not, as yet, talked about memory — perhaps readers who are already familiar with other programming languages have wondered about how to reserve vectors and arrays in LISP (as is done in BASIC, FORTRAN, ALGOL, etc.). One great advantage of LISP is that it totally relieves you of this concern. In order to quickly explain to you how this is possible, let us go back a bit.

In LISP we have lists and atoms. We have, however, mentioned the existence of dotted pairs (which we can do without, as we have done up until now). The dotted pair is represented as a box divided into two:

The dotted pair is made up of an opening bracket, any LISP object (atom, list or dotted pair), a dividing dot, another object of any sort and finally a closing bracket. The dotted pair (A . B) will be

(A . (B . C)) will be

and ((A . B) . (C,D)) will be

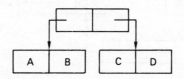

A new convention is needed.

Convention 4: Lists may be represented by a sub-collection of dotted pairs:

the list (A) will be (A . NIL)
the list (A B) will be (A . (B . NIL))
the list (A B C) will be (A . (B . (C . NIL)))

Diagrammatically

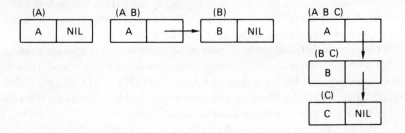

Therefore, ((A) B C) will be

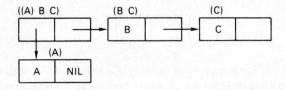

We can see straight away that the value returned when CAR is applied to a dotted pair is the object placed in the left-most (right-most when dealing with CDR) division of this dotted pair. Thus the value of (CDR '(A)) – that is, (CDR '(A . NIL)) – is, of course, NIL. CONS creates a new dotted pair, for example:

(CONS '(NON) '(EMPTY LIST)), that is
(CONS '(NON . NIL) '(EMPTY . (LIST . NIL)))

or diagrammatically

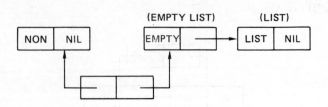

has the value ((NON) EMPTY LIST).
Consequently, (CONS 'A 'B) produces

which will be printed (in accordance with dotted pairs) as

```
?(CONS 'A 'B)
   (A . B)
```

Of course, a dotted pair will be printed in this way only if its CDR is non-NIL, otherwise it is a list and it will be printed as such. The function READ can read dotted pairs on the condition that they respect the syntax (*expression 1* . *expression 2*). Therefore, READ can read the expressions

(*term* . NIL) or (*term*)

without any problem.

■ The LISP memory comprises a collection of dotted pairs (numbered from 1 to n) as well as a collection of atoms (numbered from 1 to p). The numbers n and p represent the maximum number of dotted pairs and of atoms respectively that it is possible to use at the same time.

At any time there will be used dotted pairs (values or properties of known atoms) and unused ones. When we write

?(SET 'P '(WE LOVE LISP))
   (WE LOVE LISP)

(recalling the definition of TOPLEVEL), READ has, for example, constructed the following list (when talking about dotted pairs, we have mentioned their associated number: a dotted pair is defined by what it contains and not by its number – this means that the list remains unaltered whatever the numbers of the dotted pairs used):

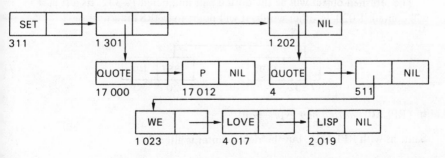

and has given it to EVAL which will return the dotted pair 1 023 – that is, the list (WE LOVE LISP), as value. After this form has been evaluated, the dotted pairs 311, 1 301, 17 000, 17 012, 1 202, 4 and 511 are useless, and are recovered by a 'garbage collection' algorithm which enables them to be used again. When building a new dotted pair, CONS forces the garbage collector to find and supply it with a free dotted pair. Therefore everything works automatically, without any problem and without any worries to the user, until all the dotted pairs are used at the same time, in which case the interpreter will stop through lack of resources.

LISP is a language of lists (the name 'LISP' comes from 'LISt Processor') but may be considered as a language of pointers, which is why there are two new primitives RPLACA and RPLACD that allow the modification of the left or right pointers of dotted pairs.

- **(RPLACA** *dotted pair expression***)**

Arguments: The value of *dotted pair* must be a dotted pair (for example, a non-empty list). *Expression* may have any value.
Value: The dotted pair (that is, the value of the first argument) with its left pointer changed so as to point to the value of the second argument.

Example

```
?(RPLACA '(CAR . CDR) '(FIRST))
   ((FIRST) . CDR)
```

or diagrammatically

The returned object will be the dotted pair numbered 17 332. Its left part will contain 1 020; in other words, it will point to (FIRST):

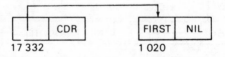

- **(RPLACD** *dotted pair expression***)**

Same as with RPLACA, but the right pointer is altered.

Example

```
?(RPLACD '((FIRST). CDR) '(REST REST))
   ((FIRST) REST REST)
```

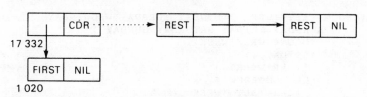

17 332

These primitives are dangerous as they can cause side-effects that are difficult to debug; for example, the function APPEND (chapter 4) concatenates two lists by recopying the first. The function NCONC directly concatenates the second list to the first.

```
?(DE NCONC (L1 L2)
?   (IF (CONSP L1)
?       (IF (CONSP (CDR L1))
?           (PROGN (NCONC (CDR L1) L2) L1)
?           (RPLACD L1 L2) )
?       L2 ) )
    NCONC
```

```
?(SET 'P '(WE LOVE))
    (WE LOVE)
?(SET 'Q '(LISP))
    (LISP)
?(NCONC P Q)
    (WE LOVE LISP)
?Q
    (LISP)
?P
    (WE LOVE LISP)
```

or diagrammatically

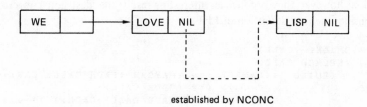

established by NCONC

NCONC avoids useless recopying but may have undesirable effects. However, NCONC (or rather RPLACD, which is used by NCONC), does enable circular lists to be built:

```
?(PROGN (SET 'WEEK '(MONDAY TUESDAY WEDNESDAY
?        THURSDAY FRIDAY SATURDAY SUNDAY ))
?        (NCONC WEEK WEEK)
?        (DE DAY ()
?           (CAR WEEK) )
?        (DE TOMORROW ()
?           (CAR (SET 'WEEK
?                      (CDR WEEK) )) )
?        (DAY) )
   MONDAY

?(TOMORROW)
   TUESDAY

?WEEK     ; alas !
   (TUESDAY WEDNESDAY THURSDAY FRIDAY SATURDAY
SUNDAY MONDAY TUESDAY WEDNESDAY THURSDAY FRIDAY
SATURDAY SUNDAY MONDAY TUESDAY ... )
```

This infinite print must be interrupted. The interpreter is actually trying to
visualise the following circular list:

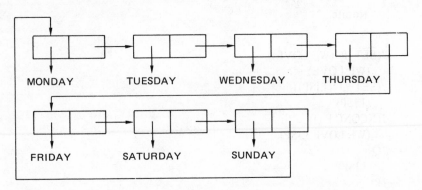

We could talk a great deal about these primitives, discussing whether their
advantages are or are not compensated by the difficulties that they cause
(implicit modification of common sub-expressions). Combined with macro-
functions however, they produce an interesting result: the 'destructive-macros'.
    Consider the new definition of LET:

```
?(DM LET (CALL)
?  (RPLACB CALL
?    (BUILD '((LAMBDA (:= (MAPCAR (CADR CALL) CAR))
?                     (:↑ (CDDR CALL)) )
?              (:↑ (MAPCAR (CADR CALL) CADR)) )) ) )
   LET

?(DE RPLACB (CELL EXP)
?  (RPLACD (RPLACA CELL (CAR EXP))
?          (CDR EXP) ) )
   RPLACB
```

```
?(SET 'E '(LET((X (CONS 'A 'B)))
?              (CAR X) ))
   (LET ((X (CONS (QUOTE A) (QUOTE B)))) (CAR X))

?(EVAL E)
   A

?E
   ((LAMBDA(X)(CAR X)) (CONS (QUOTE A) (QUOTE B)))
```

The form generated by the macro-function LET destroys the calling form (using RPLACB), which is why, if you have to evaluate E again, there will no longer be any need to call the macro-function LET again, as it has disappeared! This is the reason why we pass the entire calling expression and not just the argument list (as with an FEXPR) to a macro-function variable.

Note

For convenience when programming interpreters, the predicate EQ actually tests equality between the numbers given to objects of the same type. So it tests the equality of two atoms and also the identity of two dotted pairs:

```
?(LET ((X (CONS 'A 'B)))(EQ X X))
   T

?(EQ (CONS 'A 'B)(CONS 'A 'B))
   NIL
```

In the first case, the arguments used with EQ are one and the same dotted pair, in the second case, the arguments are two different dotted pairs. However, we might mention that certain LISP systems (although these are extremely rare) treat CONS as a real function (in the mathematical sense); in other words, they give the same result for the same arguments. In this case, the value of the second expression would be T.

8.1 Exercises

8.1.1 Write a variation of the function REVERSE, not using CONS.

9 Putting LISP into Practice

Our aim in this chapter is to present some tools (either offered by the interpreters or programmable, if unavailable) that enable programs to be tested. These tools (or functions) do not use any new concepts that have not been previously discussed.

Once your problem is solved on paper, in other words, once you have written the function definitions and the associated dry runs, the first evaluations will generally be catastrophic. You will find syntax errors (mostly missing brackets) as well as logic errors: ranging from the most basic (inverting the alternate cases in an IF expression, forgetting a terminator in a recursion) to the most subtle (bad environment management). With the facilities that are usually available, LISP allows a large range of interactions: LISP is the supreme interactive language.

Syntax errors will be avoided if you indent your expressions correctly, as does PRETTY-PRINT. In return, an accurate comparison of the original definition with the one produced by 'PRETTY-PRINT' will enable these errors to be detected. There are as many standards for writing LISP expressions as there are users and it would be pointless for us to impose our preference. PRETTY-PRINT is a function (a classic example of data driven programming) that faces the difficult problem of unfortunately having the right margin placed at a finite distance from the left margin, whereas the complexity of LISP expressions may vary.

The rest is just a question of aesthetics, knowing, for example, whether

> (IF *if then*
>   *else 1*
>   *. . .*
>   *else n*)

is more attractive than

> (IF *if*
>   *then*
>   *else 1 . . . else n*)

Logic errors are less simple to fix. They are detected mainly through the controlled execution of the suspect functions. This last point requires that, for a given function, we are able to inspect its definition. Up until now, no function, when given a function as argument, allows its definition to be returned as value. This function exists (or may be written) on all interpreters, but does not have a standardised name. We will therefore suppose that the value of FUNCTIONP, when applied to a function of type EXPR, FEXPR, NEXPR or MEXPR, is not the atom T, but the list (non-empty, therefore equivalent to T) whose first term is the atom LAMBDA, FLAMBDA, NLAMBDA or MLAMBDA, according to the function type, whose second term is the list of variables and whose following terms constitute the function body. Thus

```
?(FUNCTIONP FACT)
    (LAMBDA (N) (IF (EQ N 1) 1 (*N (FACT (SUB1 N)))))
```

The controlled execution of a function is done by modifying its definition, into which we have the choice of introducing: argument tests, tests for returned values, various printing, a call to a new interpretation loop (TOPLEVEL), etc.

On several occasions we have used the function TRACE which allows us to see the arguments and the values of named (non-anonymous) functions of type EXPR. The reader can easily extend these traces to the NEXPR, FEXPR and MEXPR functions as well as to the SUBR and FSUBR ones.

```
(DF TRACE (NAMES)
  (MAPCAR NAMES (LAMBDA(NAME)
   (IF (SYMBOLP NAME)
      (LET ((DEF (FUNCTIONP (EVAL NAME))))
          (IF (AND DEF
                    (CONSP DEF)
                    (EQ (CAR DEF) 'LAMBDA) )
               (PROGN (PUT NAME NAME (EVAL NAME))
                      (SET NAME (EVAL (BUILD '
          (LAMBDA (:= (CADR DEF))
                  (PRINT (LIST '(:= NAME) (:↑ (CADR DEF))))
                  (PRINT (PROGN (:↑ (CDDR DEF)))) ) ))) ) ) ) )) )
```

If a function had been defined as

(DE *name* (*variables*. . .) *body*. . .)

then the traced function will be defined as

(DE *name* (*variables*. . .)
    (PRINT (LIST '*name variables*. . .))
    (PRINT (PROGN *body*. . .)))

This transformation assumes that the arguments will be evaluated in the current environment (in other words, in the same environment where they would have been evaluated if the function had not been traced), that they will only be evaluated once, and that they will be given to the original function whose result will be printed when calculated.

The effect of TRACE is cancelled out by UNTRACE:

```
(DF UNTRACE (NAMES)
  (MAPCAR NAMES (LAMBDA(NAME)
   (IF (SYMBOLP NAME)
      (LET ((FN (GET NAME NAME)))
          (IF FN (SET NAME FN)) ) )) )
```

The simple trace presented above is not, in fact, the one that has been used in this book. The programming for this is a little more complex and requires two extra primitive functions.

■ (PRIN1 *expression*)

Argument: The value of *expression* must be a printable object.
Value: The atom NIL. PRIN1 prints its argument (just like PRINT) but does not jump to a new line after printing. Therefore, PRIN1 enables several objects to be printed on the same line.

Example

```
(PROGN (PRIN1 '=)(PRIN1 '=)(PRINT '=) T)
= = =
        T
```

■ (TERPRI)

Argument: None
Value: The atom NIL. TERPRI (for 'TERminate PRInt') prints any objects waiting to be printed (objects are placed in a waiting state by PRIN1 — they are only printed through the execution of TERPRI, or PRINT, or when the line is full) and jumps to the next line. If there are no objects waiting to be output, TERPRI has no effect.

Note
PRINT may be defined using PRIN1 and TERPRI:

```
?(DE PRINT (EXP)
?          (PRIN1 EXP)
?          (TERPRI)
?          EXP )
      PRINT
```

Example

```
?(PROGN (PRIN1 'START)(TERPRI)(TERPRI)
?          (PRIN1 'END) )
START
END
      NIL
```

The special LISP characters may also be printed! These characters (opening and closing brackets, dot, 'quote') may be considered as normal characters if they are immediately preceded by a special character called an escape character. The escape character is often $ (or occasionally / or !). So, if we want to print an atom whose name contains the characters '(' and ')', we write

```
?(ATOM (PRINT '$(FALSE-LIST$)))
(FALSE-LIST)
    T
```

Of course, the escape character is also a special character and must be written twice in order to be represented.

```
?(DE SNAP (A)
?    (PRIN1 A)
?    (PRIN1 '$ $=$ )      ; "$" is not necessary before "="
?    (PRINT (EVAL A)) )
    SNAP

?(SNAP (PROGN (SET 'P 3) 'P))
P = 3
    3
```

The complete trace function, as used in this book, is described as follows. If a function is defined as:

   (DE *name* (*variables*. . .) *body*. . .)

then TRACE will alter it to

   (DM *name* (CALL)
      (PUT 'TRACE '*name* (ADD1 (GET 'TRACE '*name*)))
      (CONS (LAMBDA (*variables*. . .)
        (TERPRI)
        (REPEAT (GET 'TRACE '*name*) (PRIN1 '$))
        (PRINT (LIST '*name variables*. . .))
        (PRINT (PROG1 (PROGN *body*. . .)
        (TERPRI)
        (REPEAT (GET 'TRACE '*name*)
        (PRIN1 '$))
        (PUT 'TRACE '*name* (SUB1 (GET 'TRACE '*name*)))
)
   (CDR CALL)))

Before any use of *name*, we will have made a point of evaluating:

   (PUT 'TRACE '*name* 0)

The function REPEAT allows an expression to be evaluated n times in succession:

```
(DM REPEAT (CALL)
   (CONS 'PROGN
          (REPEAT1 (EVAL (CADR CALL))
                   (CONS 'PROGN (CDDR CALL)) ) ) )
```

```
(DE REPEAT1 (N EXP)
  (IF (GT N 0)
      (CONS EXP (REPEAT1 (SUB1 N)
                         EXP )) ) )
```

For example

```
?(REPEAT1 3 '(PRIN1 '=))
   ((PRIN1 (QUOTE =)) (PRIN1 (QUOTE =)) (PRIN1 (QUOTE =)))

?(REPEAT 30 (PRIN1 '$.))
. . . . . . . . . . . . . . . . . . . . . . . . . . . . . .
   NIL
```

So, with a trace, we get correct indentations which provide improved legibility and better guidelines to connected argument — value pairs (since they start in the same column).

There are other ways of working with LISP. We will leave it up to the reader to imagine what these are, as we hope to have convinced you that adding final touches to LISP is simple, and enables you to work at the language level as well as to create all the required interactions, while having the full power of the interpreter at your disposal.

9.1 Exercises

9.1.1 Write a function LPRINT that prints its argument — list on a single line without the outer brackets.

```
?(LPRINT '(TEST OF LPRINT))
TEST OF LPRINT
  (TEST OF LPRINT)
```

9.1.2 Write the function ADVISE, which, when applied to a function of type EXPR

> (ADVISE *name before after*)

allows it to be redefined as

> (DE *name* (*variables*...)
>   (LET ((BEFORE *before*)
>   (RESULT (PROGN *body*...))
>   (AFTER *after*))
>   RESULT))

10 A Software Robot

This chapter gives to the reader a complete description of a small, software robot that has the ability to comprehend natural language (a very limited subset of the English Language), a few fragments of intelligent reasoning and finally the power of dialogue and obedience.

Most of this chapter comprises the commented program for this robot. The programming that has been done for this purpose incorporates the main styles shown in this book and, although it may be inefficient, the aim was to make it legible, modular and structured. The reader is strongly urged to somehow enrich the universe, the language or the intelligence of this robot.

The comments made will concern the algorithms, the data structures and the more difficult programming concepts, but will not explain the intimate detail of the simpler functions. These functions involve the elaboration of LISP facilities as well as examples of their use; when given suitable parameters, these facilities may be used to solve certain of the problems suggested in this book.

Let us now present one of the dialogues that you can have with the robot. This dialogue does not exhaust all the potential nor even all the possibilities of the robot, but is simply aimed at showing its most prominent features.

```
?       (ROBOT)



HELLO
JUST ASK ME PLEASE
?       (I GIVE YOU A BLUE BOX NAMED ALPHA)
THANKS FOR THE BLUE BOX (ALPHA)
JUST ASK ME PLEASE
?       (THEN I GIVE YOU A RED BOX CALLED BETA)
WAIT MY HAND IS FULL
I LAY THE BLUE BOX (ALPHA) ON THE FLOOR
THANKS FOR THE RED BOX (BETA)
JUST ASK ME PLEASE
?       (PLEASE TAKE ALPHA)
I MUST LAY THE RED BOX (BETA)
I LAY THE RED BOX (BETA) ON THE FLOOR
I TAKE THE BLUE BOX (ALPHA) IN MY HAND
JUST ASK ME PLEASE
?       (WHAT DO YOU SEE)
I LOOK AT THE BLUE BOX (ALPHA)
JUST ASK ME PLEASE
?       (PUT ALPHA ON BETA)
```

I PUT THE BLUE BOX (ALPHA) ON THE RED BOX (BETA)
JUST ASK ME PLEASE
?   (GOOD , NOW I GIVE YOU A RED SPHERE : GAMMA)
THANKS FOR THE RED SPHERE (GAMMA)
JUST ASK ME PLEASE
?   (LASTLY I GIVE YOU A SILVER PRISM : DELTA)
WAIT MY HAND IS FULL
I LAY THE RED SPHERE (GAMMA) ON THE FLOOR
THANKS FOR THE SILVER PRISM (DELTA)
JUST ASK ME PLEASE
?   (I WANT YOU TO LAY DELTA)
I LAY THE SILVER PRISM (DELTA) ON THE FLOOR
JUST ASK ME PLEASE
?   (DRINK THE PRISM)
I DO NOT REALLY UNDERSTAND
JUST ASK ME PLEASE
?   (BUT WHAT DO YOU KNOW)
I KNOW THAT :
I LOOK AT THE SILVER PRISM (DELTA)
I DO NOT HOLD ANYTHING AT ALL
THERE IS A STACK COMPOSED OF : THE SILVER PRISM (DELTA
THAT IS ALL FOR THAT STACK
THERE IS A STACK COMPOSED OF : THE RED SPHERE (GAMMA)
THAT IS ALL FOR THAT STACK
THERE IS A STACK COMPOSED OF : THE RED BOX (BETA)
UNDER THE BLUE BOX (ALPHA)
THAT IS ALL FOR THAT STACK
THAT IS ALL I KNOW
JUST ASK ME PLEASE
?   (LET US TRY : PUT GAMMA ON ALPHA)
WAIT I MUST TAKE IN MY HAND THE RED SPHERE (GAMMA)
I TAKE THE RED SPHERE (GAMMA) IN MY HAND
I PUT THE RED SPHERE (GAMMA) ON THE BLUE BOX (ALPHA)
JUST ASK ME PLEASE
?   (AND PUT DELTA ON DELTA)
YOU ARE FOOLISH !
JUST ASK ME PLEASE
?   (WHAT DO YOU KNOW)
I KNOW THAT :
I LOOK AT THE SILVER PRISM (DELTA)
I DO NOT HOLD ANYTHING AT ALL
THERE IS A STACK COMPOSED OF : THE SILVER PRISM (DELTA
THAT IS ALL FOR THAT STACK
THERE IS A STACK COMPOSED OF : THE RED BOX (BETA)
UNDER THE BLUE BOX (ALPHA)
UNDER THE RED SPHERE (GAMMA)
THAT IS ALL FOR THAT STACK
THAT IS ALL I KNOW
JUST ASK ME PLEASE
?   (MORE DIFFICULT , PUT BETA ON ALPHA)
WAIT I MUST TAKE IN MY HAND THE RED BOX (BETA)
I MUST FREE THE RED BOX (BETA)
THE BLUE BOX (ALPHA) IS ABOVE

```
I MUST FREE THE BLUE BOX (ALPHA)
THE RED SPHERE (GAMMA) IS ABOVE
I TAKE THE RED SPHERE (GAMMA) IN MY HAND
I LAY THE RED SPHERE (GAMMA) ON THE FLOOR
I TAKE THE BLUE BOX (ALPHA) IN MY HAND
I LAY THE BLUE BOX (ALPHA) ON THE FLOOR
I TAKE THE RED BOX (BETA) IN MY HAND
I PUT THE RED BOX (BETA) ON THE BLUE BOX (ALPHA)
JUST ASK ME PLEASE
?      (GIVE ME DELTA)
HUMM I MUST LOOK FOR THE SILVER PRISM (DELTA)
I TAKE THE SILVER PRISM (DELTA) IN MY HAND
I GIVE YOU BACK THE SILVER PRISM (DELTA)
JUST ASK ME PLEASE
?      (WHAT DO YOU KNOW)
I KNOW THAT :
I DO NOT LOOK AT ANYTHING IN PARTICULAR
I DO NOT HOLD ANYTHING AT ALL
THERE IS A STACK COMPOSED OF : THE BLUE BOX (ALPHA)
UNDER THE RED BOX (BETA)
THAT IS ALL FOR THAT STACK
THERE IS A STACK COMPOSED OF : THE RED SPHERE (GAMMA)
THAT IS ALL FOR THAT STACK
THAT IS ALL I KNOW
JUST ASK ME PLEASE
?      (THAT IS GOOD STOP NOW)
GOOD BYE
    NIL
```

10.1 General Concepts

The robot uses two main facilities (MICRO-MATCH and MICRO-PARSE) whose use is controlled by a database that contains facts about the universe and the actions whose execution takes place within this universe, as well as by a collection of rules that control the possible interactions between the facts and the actions in the universe.

MICRO-PARSE is a function that takes a natural language sentence (the one transmitted by the robot operator) and translates it in terms of actions.

MICRO-MATCH is a function that enables various pattern matches to be performed.

Everything is centred around the idea of a universe. As was suggested in the previous dialogue, the robot handles objects that have a shape (box, cube, sphere, etc.) and a colour (red, blue, yellow, etc.). The robot has an articulated hand that it can use to pick up or put down objects, one at a time. It can therefore build piles of objects whose base stands on infinite ground (you can always put one more object on the ground, whereas you may only put one object on to another). The robot also has a single eye. It can look at the ground or at any object in its universe. Its eye is connected to its hand in the sense that the actions 'take' and 'put' require the eye to determine the displaced object.

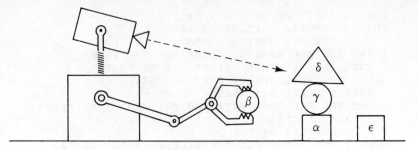

The possible robot actions within this universe are: to look at or to pick up an object, to put it down on another object or on the ground, to accept a new object given by the operator or to return one to him. Each possible action alters the universe. In order to be executed, an action requires that certain pre-suppositions are checked: after completion, the relations that exist between the eye and the hand, the ground and the objects are updated. A collection of rules code this universe. The robot's intelligence is also included in these rules in the sense that if an action cannot be executed, the obstacles are analysed and the actions to remove them are forced.

The programs that follow are sub-divided into several parts:

(1) A collection of utility functions that you can skip over on the first read.
(2) Pattern-matching functions (MICRO-MATCH).
(3) Analysis functions (MICRO-PARSE) along with the grammar that the robot recognises.
(4) Functions for database administration.
(5) Functions for linking dialogues.

Complex data will be presented in LISP form and in a more aesthetic form achieved by a function like PRETTY-PRINT. The code for these will not be given.

10.2 Utility and Complementary Functions

Various utility functions are necessary. Firstly we need a new version of BUILD. This has an extra builder *ONE* which requires an extra argument at the time of calling BUILD: this argument is an A-list and (*ONE* *identifier*) allows you to insert the value associated with *identifier* (in the A-list) within the expression to be built.

```
(DM BUILD (CALL)
   (LIST 'BUILD1
         (CADR CALL)
         (IF (CDDR CALL) (CADDR CALL)) ) )

(DE BUILD1 (L AL)
```

```
(IF (CONSP L)
    (IF (CONSP (CAR L))
        (IF (GET 'BUILD (CAAR L))
            ((GET 'BUILD (CAAR L)) L AL)
            (CONS (BUILD1 (CAR L) AL)
                  (BUILD1 (CDR L) AL) ) )
        (CONS (CAR L) (BUILD1 (CDR L) AL)) )
    L ) )

(PUT 'BUILD ':= (LAMBDA(L AL)
    (CONS (EVAL (CADAR L))
          (BUILD1 (CDR L) AL) ) ))

(PUT 'BUILD ':↑ (LAMBDA(L AL)
    (APPEND (EVAL (CADAR L))
            (BUILD1 (CDR L) AL) ) ))

(PUT 'BUILD '*ONE* (LAMBDA(L AL)
    (CONS (LET ((R (ASSOC (CADAR L) AL)))
               (IF R (CDR R) (CAR L)) )
          (BUILD1 (CDR L) AL) ) ))
```

MPRINT is a function that accepts any number of arguments and that prints them one after another, separated by spaces.

```
(DN MPRINT (L)
   (LPRINT L) )
(DE LPRINT (L)
   (IF (CONSP L)
       (PROGN (PRIN1 (CAR L))
              (PRIN1 '$ )
              (LPRINT (CDR L)) )
       (TERPRI) ) )
```

MAPC is a recursive function, similar to MAPCAR and MAPCAN except that it always returns NIL.

```
(DE MAPC (L FN)
   (IF (CONSP L)
       (PROGN (FN (CAR L))
              (MAPC (CDR L) FN) ) ) )
```

EPROGN is a variation of PROGN with preliminary evaluation of the argument:

```
(DM EPROGN (CALL)
   (CONS 'PROGN (CDR CALL)) )
```

FLAG and FLAGP allow the placement of an indicator on the P-list of an atom. We are interested in the presence of the indicator and not in its associated value (taken here to be equal to T). In LISP interpreters, FLAG and FLAGP are often primitive functions.

```
(DE FLAG (A I)
  (PUT A I T) )

(SET 'FLAGP GET)
```

The function LET that will be used here is slightly different from the one presented before. If the calling form is

> (LET ((*variable 1 value 1*)
>
>   . . .
>
>   (*variable n value n*))
>   *body.* . .)

then the generated form will be

> ((LAMBDA (SELF *variable 1 . . . variable n*)
>   *body.* . .)
> (LAMBDA (*variable 1 . . . variable n*)
>   *body.* . .)
> *value 1*
>
>   . . .
>
> *value n*)

SELF is a functional variable (connected to a function) and can therefore be applied to arguments just like a function.

The modification enables the body of LET to be called by SELF, thus producing a kind of anonymous, recursive LET. This characteristic is taken from VLISP.

```
(DM LET (CALL)
  (BUILD '((LAMBDA(SELF (:↑ (MAPCAR (CADR CALL) CAR)))
                   (:↑ (CDDR CALL)) )
          (LAMBDA (:= (MAPCAR (CADR CALL) CAR))
                   (:↑ (CDDR CALL)) )
          (:↑ (MAPCAR (CADR CALL) CADR)) )) )
```

Note

This construction allows us to dispense with auxiliary constructions; for example

```
(DE FACT (N)
  (LET ((N N)(R 1))
    (IF (LE N 1) R
        (SELF (SUB1 N) (* N R)) ) ) )
```

The function DO is another MEXPR that allows you to carry out a large series of iterations. DO is called as follows:

(DO ((*variable 1 initialisation 1 modification 1*)
　　　(*variable 2 initialisation 2 modification 2*)
　　　. . . . .
　　　(*variable n initialisation n modification n*))
　　(*test for end final value. . .*)
　　body. . .)

The corresponding generated form will be

(LET ((*variable 1 initialisation 1*)
　　　(*variable 2 initialisation 2*)
　　　. . . . .
　　　(*variable n initialisation n*))
　　(IF *test for end*
　　　　(PROGN *final value. . .*)
　　　　body. . .
　　　　(SELF *modification 1 modification 2 . . . modification n*)))

```
(DM DO (CALL)
   (BUILD '(LET (:= (MAPCAR (CADR CALL)
                            (LAMBDA(P)(LIST (CAR P)
                                           (CADR P) )) ))
            (IF (:= (CAADDR CALL))
                (PROGN (:↑ (CDADDR CALL)))
                (:↑ (CDDDR CALL))
                (SELF (:↑ (MAPCAR (CADR CALL)
                                  CADDR))) ) )) )
```

Example
The previous factorial function may be written as

```
(DE FACT (N)
   (DO ((N N (SUB1 N))
        (R 1 (* N R)) )
       ((LE N 1) R) ) )
```

You will notice that in the use of DO above, there is no body. This construction is taken from MACLISP.

10.3 Pattern Matching

Pattern matching is a technique that allows you to strip a list down according to a pre-determined framework, in order to extract the parts of interest. For example, if we wish:

(1) to check that a list comprises a term, which is itself composed of two terms, the first of which is the atom HAND

(2) to be able to recover the CADR of this same term with a view to future use

we write

> (MICRO-MATCH 'list '(?- (HAND ! X) ?-)† T)

In the case of failure the reply will be NIL (in other words, if there is no term whose CAR is HAND or, if there is, either because the CDR of this term is NIL, or because the CDDR is not NIL); in the case of success, the environment will be

> ((X . CADR *of the first term whose* CAR *is* HAND) . T)

By using the function ASSOC, we can find the 'value' associated with the 'pattern-matching variable': X in this environment.

The function MICRO-MATCH takes three arguments: an expression, a pattern and an environment (an A-list) and returns an environment or NIL if unsuccessful.

A pattern is either an atom, in which case it can only be successfully matched with itself, or a list of patterns, and in this case it can only be matched with a list where each term is successfully matched with the corresponding pattern in the pattern list. A pattern may also be considered as special. There are three special patterns:

(1) (*ONE*) is matched with any object. This pattern is abbreviated to !-.
(*ONE* *identifier*) is matched with any object, but in addition it associates the matched value with the pattern-matching variable *identifier*. This variable may be re-used later on to match the same value. This pattern is abbreviated to !*identifier*.

(2) (*ANY*) is matched with any sequence of any objects. It is abbreviated to ?-

(3) (*LIST-WHERE-MUST-BE* *patterns*. . .) is only successfully matched with a list that contains, for each pattern present in *patterns*. . ., a term that can be matched with this pattern.

More formally, a pattern is defined by the following relations:

> *pattern* = *atom*
> or (*pattern pattern*. . .*pattern*)
> or (*ONE*)
> or (*ONE**identifier*)
> or (*ANY*)
> or (*LIST-WHERE-MUST-BE* *pattern pattern* . . . *pattern*)

---

† ?-, !- and !*identifier* are abbreviations for (*ANY*), (*ONE*) and (*ONE**identifier*), just as '*expression* is an abbreviation for (QUOTE *expression*).

Examples

```
?(MICRO-MATCH '(A A) '(!X !X) T)
  ((X . A) . T)

?(MICRO-MATCH '(A B) '(!X !X) T)
    NIL

(MICRO-MATCH '(3 1 4 1 5 9) '(3 ?- !X ?- !X ?-) T)
  ((X . 1) . T)
```

The list in the last example is matched as

The function **MICRO-MATCH** is an example of data driven programming (in this case, the pattern).

```
(DE MICRO-MATCH (E F AL)
  (IF AL
      (IF (ATOM F)
          (IF (EQ E F) AL)
          (LET ((FN (GET 'MICRO-MATCH (CAR F))))
              (IF FN (FN E F AL)
                     (MICRO-MATCH-LIST E F AL) ) ) ) ) )

; pattern (*ONE*) or (*ONE* x)

(PUT 'MICRO-MATCH '*ONE* (LAMBDA (E F AL)
  (IF (NULL (CDR F))
      AL
      (LET ((V (ASSOC (CADR F) AL)))
          (IF V
              (IF (EQUAL E (CDR V)) AL)
              (CONS (CONS (CADR F) E)
                    AL ) ) ) ) ))

(DE MICRO-MATCH-LIST (E F AL)
  (IF AL
      (IF (CONSP F)
          (IF (CONSP (CAR F))
              (LET ((FN (GET 'MICRO-MATCH-LIST (CAAR F))))
                  (IF FN (FN E F AL)
                      (IF (CONSP E)
                          (MICRO-MATCH-LIST (CDR E)
                                            (CDR F)
                                            (MICRO-MATCH (CAR E)
                                                         (CAR F)
                                                         AL )
                          ) ) ) )
              (IF (CONSP E)
                  (MICRO-MATCH-LIST (CDR E)
                                    (CDR F)
                                    (MICRO-MATCH (CAR E)
                                                 (CAR F)
                                                 AL ) ) ) )
          (IF (EQ E F) AL) ) ) )
```

```
; pattern (*ANY*)

(PUT 'MICRO-MATCH-LIST '*ANY* (LAMBDA (E F AL)
    (IF (NULL (CDR F)) AL
        (IF (CONSP E)
            (OR (MICRO-MATCH-LIST E (CDR F) AL)
                (MICRO-MATCH-LIST (CDR E) F AL) )
            (MICRO-MATCH-LIST E (CDR F) AL) ) ) ))

; pattern (*LIST-WHERE-MUST-BE* x y z ...)

(PUT 'MICRO-MATCH '*LIST-WHERE-MUST-BE* (LAMBDA (E F AL)
    (IF (CDR F)
        (MICRO-MATCH E
                     (CONS '*LIST-WHERE-MUST-BE*
                           (CDDR F) )
                     (MICRO-MATCH-LIST E
                                       (LIST '(*ANY*)
                                             (CADR F)
                                             '(*ANY*) )
                                       AL ) )
        AL ) ))
```

10.4   Natural Language Interface

The function MICRO-PARSE takes two arguments: a sentence and a grammar.
It returns a synthesised value which corresponds to the input sentence analysed
according to the grammar. If the analysis is impossible, NIL is returned as the
value. The grammar is formally described as follows:

> *grammar* = (*rule rule . . . rule*)
> with:
> *rule*   = (*form value to synthesise*)
> *form* is a pattern suitable to be used by MICRO-MATCH;
> *value to synthesise* is a constructor to be used by BUILD.

Example
When compared with the form (?- TAKE !X ?-), the sentence (PLEASE TAKE
ALPHA WHICH IS THERE IN FRONT OF YOU) will enable X and ALPHA to
be associated in order to build the clause (WANT-TO-TAKE ALPHA).

```
(DE MICRO-PARSE (EXP GRAMMAR)
  (IF GRAMMAR
      (LET ((R (MICRO-MATCH EXP (CAAR GRAMMAR) T)))
           (IF R (BUILD (CADAR GRAMMAR) R)
               (MICRO-PARSE EXP (CDR GRAMMAR)) ) ) ) )


(SET 'ROBOT-GRAMMAR '(
(((*ANY*) I GIVE YOU (*ONE*) (*ONE*COLOR) (*ONE* TYPE)
                     (*ONE*) (*ONE* X) (*ANY*) )
 (WANT-TO-GIVE (*ONE* X) (*ONE* TYPE) (*ONE* COLOR)) )
(((*ANY*) GIVE ME (*ONE* X) (*ANY*))
 (WANT-TO-RETRIEVE (*ONE* X)) )
(((*ANY*) TAKE (*ONE* X) (*ANY*))
 (WANT-TO-TAKE (*ONE* X)) )
```

```
(((*ANY*) LAY (*ONE* X) (*ANY*))
 (WANT-TO-LAY (*ONE* X) FLOOR) )
(((*ANY*) PUT (*ONE* X) ON (*ONE* Y) (*ANY*))
 (WANT-TO-LAY (*ONE* X) (*ONE* Y)) )
(((*ANY*) LOOK AT (*ONE* X) (*ANY*))
 (WANT-TO-SEE (*ONE* X)) )
(((*ANY*) WHAT DO YOU KNOW (*ANY*))
 (WHAT-IS-KNOWN) )
(((*ANY*) WHAT DO YOU SEE (*ANY*))
 (WHAT-IS-SEEN) )
(((*ANY*) WHAT DO YOU HOLD (*ANY*))
 (WHAT-IS-HELD) )
(((*ANY*) STOP (*ANY*))
 (WANT-TO-STOP) )
 ))
```

The grammar is represented better in the following form:

```
?- I GIVE YOU !- !COLOR !TYPE !- !X ?-
---> (WANT-TO-GIVE !X !TYPE !COLOR)

?- GIVE ME !X ?-
---> (WANT-TO-RETRIEVE !X)

?- TAKE !X ?-
---> (WANT-TO-TAKE !X)

?- LAY !X ?-
---> (WANT-TO-LAY !X FLOOR)

?- PUT !X ON !Y ?-
---> (WANT-TO-LAY !X !Y)

?- LOOK AT !X ?-
---> (WANT-TO-SEE !X)

?- WHAT DO YOU KNOW ?-
---> (WHAT-IS-KNOWN)

?- WHAT DO YOU SEE ?-
---> (WHAT-IS-SEEN)

?- WHAT DO YOU HOLD ?-
---> (WHAT-IS-HELD)

?- STOP ?-
---> (WANT-TO-STOP)
```

There are two simple possibilities open to the user to improve the robot's command interface (in other words, to allow it to recognise more sentences more intelligently):

(1) add some new rules to the MICRO-PARSE grammar
(2) improve MICRO-MATCH by introducing some new, special patterns
(for example, *OR* which enables a word to be recognised in a list, etc.).

10.5   Database Administration

The database is made up of an ordered collection of clauses, of which we can distinguish two types:

(1) clauses indicating the actions to undertake
(2) clauses describing the state of the universe.

These clauses are all represented by lists whose first term is an atom that acts as a keyword and that identifies the clause type.

There are six clauses that describe the state of the universe:

(TYPE   *object identifier   object form*)
(COLOR *object identifier   object colour*)
(ON   *object identifier*   FLOOR)
(ON   *object identifier   object identifier*)
(HAND   *object identifier*)
(EYE   *object identifier*)

All the objects in the universe (those that are given explicitly to the robot) must have a unique name so that they may be distinguished even in the situation where the form and the colour are the same. This unique name is the *object identifier*. The TYPE and COLOR clauses determine an object's form and colour respectively. The ON clause determines an object's position. The HAND and EYE clauses determine the objects held and looked at by the robot.

Example
The clauses associated with the diagram in section 10.1 are:

```
(EYE DELTA)(HAND BETA)
(ON DELTA GAMMA)(ON GAMMA ALPHA)(ON ALPHA FLOOR)
(ON EPSILON FLOOR)
(TYPE ALPHA BOX)(COLOR ALPHA RED)
(TYPE BETA SPHERE)(COLOR BETA RED)
(TYPE GAMMA SPHERE)(COLOR GAMMA YELLOW)
(TYPE DELTA PRISM)(COLOR DELTA PURPLE)
(TYPE EPSILON BOX)(COLOR EPSILON RED)
```

There are two types of action clauses. The first type is knowledge clauses, namely

(WHAT-IS-KNOWN)
(WHAT-IS-SEEN)
(WHAT-IS-HELD)

Their execution causes the robot to describe what it knows, sees or holds (their name is prefixed by 'WHAT-IS-').

The second type of clauses deals with actions and comprises:

(WANT-TO-GIVE   *object identifier object form colour*)
(WANT-TO-RETRIEVE *object identifier*)
(WANT-TO-TAKE   *object identifier*)
(WANT-TO-LAY   *object identifier* FLOOR)
(WANT-TO-LAY   *object identifier object identifier*)
(WANT-TO-SEE   *object identifier*)
(WANT-TO-STOP)
(WANT-TO-OBEY)

These clauses correspond to the following actions:

(1) accept an object from the user
(2) return one to him
(3) pick one up
(4) put one down on the ground or on another object
(5) look at an object
(6) stop
(7) request a new order.

As you see, the name of these clauses is prefixed by 'WANT-TO'. Clauses that represent actions are placed at the head of the database, in other words, before the clauses that describe the state of the universe. The database is represented as a list of clauses, prefixed by the atom DATA and is found to be the value of this same atom: DATA. To start with, the database contains only the clause (WANT-TO-OBEY). It is initialised as follows:

```
?(PROGN (SET 'DATA (LIST 'DATA))
?        (/ADD/ (WANT-TO-OBEY)) )
  (DATA (WANT-TO-OBEY))
```

More formally:

  database = (DATA *action clauses . . . state clauses . . .*)

The reason for the presence of the atom DATA at the head of the list of clauses will be given with the function /DELETE/.

There are nine functions, five of which are more important than the other four. These five are used to handle the database: each function (apart from /FORGET/ which has no argument) is written in two ways (EXPR and FEXPR, the latter being more useful for writing behaviour rules for the robot).

/ADD/ adds a clause to the database. If the clause is an action clause it is added at the head of the action clauses; otherwise it is added at the tail of the state clauses.

/DELETE/ removes the argument clause from the base. The algorithm used by /DELETE/ does not distinguish the deletion of the first clause in the base as a special case. The reader may prove this by writing /DELETE/ where the database is represented as a list (possibly empty) of clauses.

/FORGET/ enables the first clause in the base to be deleted, whatever it may be. /FORGET/ is much quicker than /DELETE/ when removing the current action clause. But on the other hand, it is always possible to dispense with /FORGET/ by using /DELETE/.

/ERASE/ deletes a clause which is specified by its single keyword. For example

(/ERASE/ (EYE))
(/ERASE/ (EYE *object identifier*))

both delete the first clause (EYE *anything.* . .) present in the base.

/UPDATE/ allows you to update (or possibly to create) a clause that is specified by its keyword. For example

(/UPDATE/ (EYE ALPHA))

alters the first clause (EYE *anything.* . .) to (EYE ALPHA).

These five functions operate by physically altering the database so as not to perform useless recopying (direct or indirect calls to CONS).

```
(DE /E-ERASE/ (CLAUSE)
  (SET 'DATA
       (LET ((CLAUSES DATA))
            (IF (CDR CLAUSES)
                (IF (EQUAL (CAADR CLAUSES) (CAR CLAUSE))
                    (PROGN (RPLACD CLAUSES (CDDR CLAUSES))
                           DATA )
                    (SELF (CDR CLAUSES)) )
                DATA ) ) ))

(DE /E-UPDATE/ (CLAUSE)
  (SET 'DATA
       (LET ((CLAUSES DATA))
            (IF (CDR CLAUSES)
                (IF (EQUAL (CAADR CLAUSES) (CAR CLAUSE))
                    (PROGN (RPLACD (CADR CLAUSES) (CDR CLAUSE))
                           DATA )
                    (SELF (CDR CLAUSES)) )
                (/E-ADD/ CLAUSE) ) ) ) )

(DE /FORGET/ ()
  (SET 'DATA (CONS 'DATA (CDDR DATA))) )

(DE /E-ADD/ (CLAUSE)
  (SET 'DATA
       (IF (OR (GET 'RULES (CAR CLAUSE))
               (GET 'ACTION (CAR CLAUSE)) )
           (RPLACD DATA (CONS CLAUSE (CDR DATA)))
           (NCONC DATA (LIST CLAUSE)) ) ) )
```

```
(DE /E-DELETE/ (CLAUSE)
  (SET 'DATA
       (LET ((CLAUSES DATA))
            (IF (CDR CLAUSES)
                (IF (EQUAL (CADR CLAUSES) CLAUSE)
                    (PROGN (RPLACD CLAUSES (CDDR CLAUSES))
                           DATA)
                    (SELF (CDR CLAUSES)) )
                (MPRINT '***** '/DELETE/
                        CLAUSE 'WITH DATA 'IMPOSSIBLE )
                (LIST 'DATA) ) ) ))

(DF /ERASE/ (ARGS)
  (/E-ERASE/ (CAR ARGS)) )

(DF /UPDATE/ (ARGS)
  (/E-UPDATE/ (CAR ARGS)) )

(DF /ADD/ (ARGS)
  (/E-ADD/ (CAR ARGS)) )

(DF /DELETE/ (ARGS)
  (/E-DELETE/ (CAR ARGS)) )
```

10.6   The Sequencing of Dialogues

Process sequencing is performed by the function RUN-CLAUSES. The action clauses are executed in sequence by the robot. The latter distinguishes between action clauses and state clauses by the presence of the atom, which denotes the clause type, on the P-list of the atoms RULES or ACTION. There are two cases to consider.

The case of the clauses belonging to the P-list of ACTION

RUN-CLAUSES starts the function (without any arguments) associated with the keyword of the considered clause. Only two clauses are defined in this way: WANT-TO-STOP and WANT-TO-OBEY. This last clause initiates the acquisition of an order from the operator and adds the corresponding action clause (built by MICRO-PARSE).

The case of the clauses belonging to the P-list of RULES

Associated with the keyword is the list of rules that may be applied. The rules are structured as follows:

rule = ((*calling clause   context clauses. . .*)
        expressions. . .)

expressions. . . is any sequence of LISP expressions, most often consisting of calls to the handling functions (/ADD/, /DELETE/, etc.). Here is an example of a rule:

```
(((WANT-TO-TAKE ! X)    ;   calling clause
  (HAND ! X))           ;   single context clause
 (ANSWER BUT I ALREADY HAVE ! X IN MY HAND)
 (/FORGET/))
```

This rule stipulates that if the action to be executed concerns picking up an
object (WANT-TO-TAKE ! X) and this object is already in the robot's hand
(HAND ! X), then the robot must reply 'but I already have *object* in my hand'
and must then forget the clause to be executed in order to attend to what comes
next. To be more precise if, for example, we have the following situation

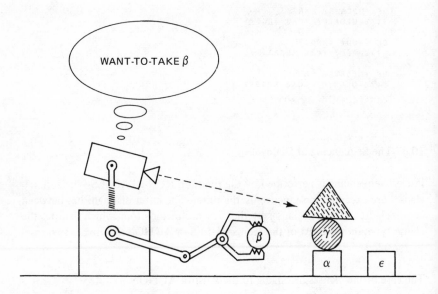

and we inquire as to whether the clause (HAND BETA) is in context, then since
it is, we evaluate (after instantiation):

> (PROGN (ANSWER BUT I ALREADY HAVE BETA IN MY HAND)
>   (/FORGET/))

This means that the robot's reply to the operator is

> 'BUT I ALREADY HAVE THE RED SPHERE (BETA) IN MY HAND'

The function ANSWER allows the robot to address the user. Instead of *object
identifier*, ANSWER substitutes the sequence:

> 'THE *object colour object form (object identifier)*'

which appears in the sentence produced.

ANSWER recognises an atom to be an *object identifier* by its presence on
the P-list of the atom OBJECT.

```
(DF ANSWER (SENTENCE)
    (LET ((SENTENCE SENTENCE))
        (IF SENTENCE
            (IF (FLAGP 'OBJECT (CAR SENTENCE))
                (PROGN (LET (
        (R (MICRO-MATCH DATA
                (BUILD '(*LIST-WHERE-MUST-BE*
                        (TYPE (:= (CAR SENTENCE))
                            (*ONE* T) )
                        (COLOR (:= (CAR SENTENCE))
                            (*ONE* C) ) ))
            T )) )
                (IF R
                    (PROGN (PRIN1 'THE)
                        (PRIN1 '$ )
                        (PRIN1 (CDR (ASSOC 'C R)))
                        (PRIN1 '$ )
                        (PRIN1 (CDR (ASSOC 'T R)))
                        (PRIN1 '$ )
                        (PRIN1 (LIST (CAR SENTENCE)))
                        (PRIN1 '$ ) )
                    (TERPRI)
                    (MPRINT '***** 'OBJECT
                            (CAR SENTENCE) 'INCORRECT
                            'IN DATA ) ) )
                (SELF (CDR SENTENCE)) )
            (IF (EQ (CAR SENTENCE) 'FLOOR)
                (PROGN (PRIN1 'THE)
                    (PRIN1 '$ )
                    (PRIN1 'FLOOR)
                    (PRIN1 '$ )
                    (SELF (CDR SENTENCE)) )
                (PRIN1 (CAR SENTENCE))
                (PRIN1 '$ )
                (SELF (CDR SENTENCE)) ) ) ) )
    (TERPRI) )
```

The order of the rules is important. The rules are applied in the order in which they appear on the list placed in the P-list of RULES. For example, the rules defining WHAT-IS-HELD are

```
(((WHAT-IS-HELD)
    (HAND (*ONE* X)) )
  (/FORGET/)
  (ANSWER I HOLD (*ONE* X)) )
(((WHAT-IS-HELD))
  (/FORGET/)
  (ANSWER I DO NOT HOLD ANYTHING AT ALL) )
```

In actual fact, these two rules correspond to:

Either the robot is holding an object
Then reply that it is holding this object
Else reply that it is not holding anything at all.

In all cases, delete the order (by using /FORGET/).

Inverting these two rules would always cause the robot to declare that it is not holding anything, the second rule always being applied since it has no context clause.

```
(DE RUN-CLAUSES ()
  (DO ()
      ((OR (NULL (CDR DATA))
           (EQ (CAADR DATA) 'WANT-TO-STOP1) ))
      (LET ((RULES (GET 'RULES (CAADR DATA))))
           (IF RULES
               (DO ((RULES RULES (CDR RULES)))
                   ((IF RULES (APPLY-RULE (CAR RULES))
                              (MPRINT '***** 'NO 'RULE
                                             'FOR (CADR DATA)
                                             'IN DATA )
                              (/FORGET/)
                              T )) )
               (LET ((ACTION (GET 'ACTION (CAADR DATA))))
                    (IF ACTION (ACTION)
                        (MPRINT '***** 'NO 'MEANING
                                       'ASSOCIATED 'TO
                                       (CADR DATA) 'IN DATA )
                        (/FORGET/) ) ) ) ) ) ) )

(DE APPLY-RULE (RULE)
    (LET ((R (MICRO-MATCH (CADR DATA) (CAAR RULE) T)))
         (IF R
             (LET ((RR (MICRO-MATCH (CDDR DATA)
                                    (CONS '*LIST-WHERE-MUST-BE*
                                          (CDAR RULE) )
                                    R )))
                  (IF RR
                      (PROGN (EPROGN (BUILD (CDR RULE) RR))
                             T ) ) ) ) ) ) )

(DE ROBOT ()
    (SET 'DATA (LIST 'DATA))
    (/ADD/ (WANT-TO-OBEY))
    (PRINT 'HELLO)
    (RUN-CLAUSES) )
```

10.7 List of Rules

The clause (WANT-TO-STOP1) stops the robot. This clause is introduced following the evaluation of (WANT-TO-STOP) by RUN-CLAUSES through the synthesis of the sentence 'Stop'.

```
(PUT 'ACTION 'WANT-TO-STOP (LAMBDA()
  (ANSWER GOOD BYE)
  (/FORGET/)
  (SET 'DATA (CONS 'DATA (CONS '(WANT-TO-STOP1)
                               (CDR DATA) ))) ))

(PUT 'ACTION 'WANT-TO-OBEY (LAMBDA()
  (LPRINT '(JUST ASK ME PLEASE))
  (LET ((CLAUSE (MICRO-PARSE (READ) ROBOT-GRAMMAR)))
       (IF CLAUSE (PROGN (/E-ADD/ CLAUSE)
                         (IF (EQ (CAR CLAUSE) 'WANT-TO-GIVE)
                             (FLAG 'OBJECT (CADR CLAUSE)) ) )
                  (LPRINT '(I DO NOT REALLY UNDERSTAND)) ) ) ))
```

The following rules are listed as printed by the functions PRETTY-PRINT-RULES and its associates. The sentences produced by ANSWER for each rule explain them sufficiently for us just to give general comments.

The robot may only receive an object if his hand is free, otherwise he puts the object he is holding down on the ground in order to free his hand. He may only return an object if he has previously taken hold of it. To pick up an object, the robot tests whether he already has it in his hand, whether his hand is empty and whether there is nothing on top of the required object. To put one object upon another or on the ground, the robot must check that he has hold of the correct object and that the top of the receiving object is free.

The clause (WHAT-IS-KNOWN) generates the clauses (which replace it) (WHAT-IS-KNOWN1 *object 1*) (WHAT-IS-KNOWN1 *object 2*). . . where all the objects i are on the ground: these are the bases of piles that exist in the universe. The rules concerning WHAT-IS-KNOWN2 explain these piles. These two clause types have been introduced in order to show the programming of two nested loops, using rules:

> for every pile
> > for every element of the pile
> > > print its description

A direct use of DATA, invoked by WHAT-IS-KNOWN, would, of course, have been possible and certainly more efficient.

The continuous clause, WANT-TO-OBEY, enables us to set up a communication loop: requesting new orders from the user and converting these orders into action clauses to execute. The loop is interrupted by (WANT-TO-STOP).

```
((LAMBDA (L)
   (MAPC L (LAMBDA (R)(PUT 'RULES
                          (CAR R)
                          (CDR R) ))) )
  '(
(WANT-TO-GIVE
   (((WANT-TO-GIVE (*ONE* X) (*ONE* T) (*ONE* C))
     (HAND (*ONE* Y)) )
    (/ADD/ (WANT-TO-LAY (*ONE* Y) FLOOR))
    (ANSWER WAIT MY HAND IS FULL) )
   (((WANT-TO-GIVE (*ONE* X) (*ONE* T) (*ONE* C)))
    (/FORGET/)
    (/ADD/ (TYPE (*ONE* X) (*ONE* T)))
    (/ADD/ (COLOR (*ONE* X) (*ONE* C)))
    (/ADD/ (HAND (*ONE* X)))
    (/UPDATE/ (EYE (*ONE* X)))
    (ANSWER THANKS FOR (*ONE* X)) )
                    )

(WANT-TO-RETRIEVE
   (((WANT-TO-RETRIEVE (*ONE* X))
     (HAND (*ONE* X))
     (TYPE (*ONE* X) (*ONE* T))
     (COLOR (*ONE* X) (*ONE* C)) )
```

```
              (ANSWER I GIVE YOU BACK (*ONE* X))
              (/ERASE/ (EYE))
              (/FORGET/)
              (/DELETE/ (HAND (*ONE* X)))
              (/DELETE/ (TYPE (*ONE* X) (*ONE* T)))
              (/DELETE/ (COLOR (*ONE* X) (*ONE* C))) )
          (((WANT-TO-RETRIEVE (*ONE* X)))
              (/ADD/ (WANT-TO-TAKE (*ONE* X)))
              (ANSWER HUMM I MUST LOOK FOR (*ONE* X)) )
                       )

      (WANT-TO-TAKE
          (((WANT-TO-TAKE (*ONE* X))
            (HAND (*ONE* X)) )
              (/FORGET/)
              (ANSWER BUT I ALREADY HAVE (*ONE* X) IN MY HAND) )
          (((WANT-TO-TAKE (*ONE* X))
            (HAND (*ONE* Y)) )
              (/ADD/ (WANT-TO-LAY (*ONE* Y) FLOOR))
              (ANSWER I MUST LAY (*ONE* Y)) )
          (((WANT-TO-TAKE (*ONE* X))
            (ON (*ONE* Y) (*ONE* X)) )
              (/ADD/ (WANT-TO-LAY (*ONE* Y) FLOOR))
              (/ADD/ (WANT-TO-TAKE (*ONE* Y)))
              (ANSWER I MUST FREE (*ONE* X))
              (ANSWER  (*ONE* Y) IS ABOVE) )
          (((WANT-TO-TAKE (*ONE* X))
            (ON (*ONE* X) (*ONE* Y)) )
              (/FORGET/)
              (/DELETE/ (ON (*ONE* X) (*ONE* Y)))
              (ANSWER I TAKE (*ONE* X) IN MY HAND)
              (/UPDATE/ (EYE (*ONE* X)))
              (/ADD/ (HAND (*ONE* X))) )
                       )

      (WANT-TO-LAY
          (((WANT-TO-LAY (*ONE* X) (*ONE* X)))
              (/FORGET/)
              (/UPDATE/ (EYE (*ONE* X)))
              (ANSWER YOU ARE FOOLISH $!) )
          (((WANT-TO-LAY (*ONE* X) (*ONE*  Y))
            (ON (*ONE* X) (*ONE* Y)) )
              (ANSWER BUT (*ONE* X) IS ALREADY ON (*ONE* Y))
              (/FORGET/) )
          (((WANT-TO-LAY (*ONE* X) FLOOR)
            (HAND (*ONE* X)) )
              (/FORGET/)
              (/UPDATE/ (EYE (*ONE* X)))
              (/DELETE/ (HAND (*ONE* X)))
              (/ADD/ (ON (*ONE* X) FLOOR))
              (ANSWER I LAY (*ONE* X) ON THE FLOOR) )
          (((WANT-TO-LAY (*ONE* X) (*ONE*  Y))
            (HAND (*ONE* X))
            (ON (*ONE* Z) (*ONE* Y)) )
              (/ADD/ (WANT-TO-LAY (*ONE* Z) FLOOR))
              (ANSWER I MUST FREE (*ONE* Y) OF (*ONE* Z)) )
          (((WANT-TO-LAY (*ONE* X) (*ONE* Y))
```

```
        (HAND (*ONE* X)) )
     (/FORGET/)
     (/UPDATE/ (EYE (*ONE* X)))
     (/DELETE/ (HAND (*ONE* X)))
     (/ADD/ (ON (*ONE* X) (*ONE* Y)))
     (ANSWER I PUT (*ONE* X) ON (*ONE* Y)) )
   (((WANT-TO-LAY (*ONE* X) (*ONE* Y))
      (HAND (*ONE* Z)) )
     (/ADD/ (WANT-TO-LAY (*ONE* Z) FLOOR))
     (ANSWER I LAY (*ONE* Z) WHICH BOTHERS ME) )
   (((WANT-TO-LAY (*ONE* X) (*ONE* Y)))
     (ANSWER WAIT I MUST TAKE IN MY HAND (*ONE* X))
     (/ADD/ (WANT-TO-TAKE (*ONE* X))) )
              )


(WHAT-IS-HELD
   (((WHAT-IS-HELD)
     (HAND (*ONE* X)) )
     (/FORGET/)
     (ANSWER I HOLD (*ONE* X)) )
   (((WHAT-IS-HELD))
     (/FORGET/)
     (ANSWER I DO NOT HOLD ANYTHING AT ALL) )
              )


(WHAT-IS-KNOWN
   (((WHAT-IS-KNOWN))
     (/FORGET/)
     (ANSWER I KNOW THAT : )
     (/ADD/ (WHAT-IS-KNOWN1))
     (MAPC DATA (LAMBDA(CLAUSE)
       (LET ((R (MICRO-MATCH CLAUSE
                            '(ON (*ONE* X) FLOOR)
                            T )))
            (IF R (/E-ADD/ (LIST 'WHAT-IS-KNOWN1
                                 (CDR (ASSOC 'X R))
                                 ))) ) ))
     (/ADD/ (WHAT-IS-HELD))
     (/ADD/ (WHAT-IS-SEEN)) )
        )


(WHAT-IS-KNOWN1
   (((WHAT-IS-KNOWN1 (*ONE* X)))
     (/ADD/ (WHAT-IS-KNOWN2 (*ONE* X)))
     (ANSWER THERE IS A STACK COMPOSED OF : (*ONE* X)) )
   (((WHAT-IS-KNOWN1 ))
     (/FORGET/)
     (ANSWER THAT IS ALL I KNOW ) )
         )


(WHAT-IS-KNOWN2
   (((WHAT-IS-KNOWN2 (*ONE* X))
     (ON (*ONE* Y) (*ONE* X)) )
     (/UPDATE/ (WHAT-IS-KNOWN2 (*ONE* Y)))
     (ANSWER UNDER (*ONE* Y)) )
   (((WHAT-IS-KNOWN2 (*ONE* X)) )
     (/FORGET/)
     (ANSWER THAT IS ALL FOR THAT STACK) )
              )
```

```
(WHAT-IS-SEEN
   (((WHAT-IS-SEEN)
     (EYE (*ONE* X)) )
    (/FORGET/)
    (ANSWER I LOOK AT (*ONE* X)))
   (((WHAT-IS-SEEN))
    (/FORGET/)
    (ANSWER I DO NOT LOOK AT ANYTHING IN PARTICULAR) )
          )
(WANT-TO-SEE
   (((WANT-TO-SEE (*ONE* X)))
    (/UPDATE/ (EYE (*ONE* X)))
    (/FORGET/)
    (ANSWER I LOOK AT (*ONE* X)) )
         )
     )))))))))))))


(WHAT-IS-KNOWN)
......
::)(/FORGET/)
   (ANSWER I KNOW THAT :)
   (/ADD/ (WHAT-IS-KNOWN1))
   (MAPC DATA
          (LAMBDA (CLAUSE)
                  (LET ((R (MICRO-MATCH CLAUSE
                                        '(ON !X
                                              FLOOR )
                                     T )))
                      (IF R
                          (/E-ADD/ (LIST 'WHAT-IS-KNOWN1
                                          (CDR (ASSOC 'X
                                                      R ))
                      ) ) ) )
   (/ADD/ (WHAT-IS-HELD))
   (/ADD/ (WHAT-IS-SEEN))
(WHAT-IS-KNOWN1 !X)
......
::)(/FORGET/)
   (/ADD/ (WHAT-IS-KNOWN2 !X))
   (ANSWER THERE IS A STACK COMPOSED OF : !X)

(WHAT-IS-KNOWN1)
......
::)(/FORGET/)
   (ANSWER THAT IS ALL I KNOW)

(WHAT-IS-KNOWN2 !X)
... (ON !Y !X)...
::)(/UPDATE/ (WHAT-IS-KNOWN2 !Y))
   (ANSWER UNDER !Y)

(WHAT-IS-KNOWN2 !X)
......
::)(/FORGET/)
   (ANSWER THAT IS ALL FOR THAT STACK)
```

```
<WHAT-IS-SEEN>
... <EYE !X>...
::>(/FORGET/)
  (ANSWER I LOOK AT !X)


<WHAT-IS-SEEN>
......
::>(/FORGET/)
  (ANSWER I DO NOT LOOK AT ANYTHING IN PARTICULAR)

<WHAT-IS-HELD>
... <HAND !X>...
::>(/FORGET/)
  (ANSWER I HOLD !X)


<WHAT-IS-HELD>
......
::>(/FORGET/)
  (ANSWER I DO NOT HOLD ANYTHING AT ALL)
<WANT-TO-GIVE !X !T !C>
... <HAND !Y>...
::>(/ADD/ (WANT-TO-LAY !Y FLOOR))
  (ANSWER WAIT MY HAND IS FULL)


<WANT-TO-GIVE !X !T !C>
......
::>(/FORGET/)
  (/ADD/ (TYPE !X !T))
  (/ADD/ (COLOR !X !C))
  (/ADD/ (HAND !X))
  (/UPDATE/ (EYE !X))
  (ANSWER THANKS FOR !X)

<WANT-TO-RETRIEVE !X>
... <HAND !X> <TYPE !X !T> <COLOR !X !C>...
::>(ANSWER I GIVE YOU BACK !X)
  (/ERASE/ (EYE))
  (/FORGET/)
  (/DELETE/ (HAND !X))
  (/DELETE/ (TYPE !X !T))
  (/DELETE/ (COLOR !X !C))

<WANT-TO-RETRIEVE !X>
......
::>(/ADD/ (WANT-TO-TAKE !X))
  (ANSWER HUMM I MUST LOOK FOR !X)

<WANT-TO-TAKE !X>
... <HAND !X>...
::>(/FORGET/)
  (ANSWER BUT I ALREADY HAVE !X IN MY HAND)

<WANT-TO-TAKE !X>
... <HAND !Y>...
::>(/ADD/ (WANT-TO-LAY !Y FLOOR))
  (ANSWER I MUST LAY !Y)
```

```
<WANT-TO-TAKE !X>
... <ON !Y !X>...
::)(/ADD/ (WANT-TO-LAY !Y FLOOR))
   (/ADD/ (WANT-TO-TAKE !Y))
   (ANSWER I MUST FREE !X)
   (ANSWER  !Y IS ABOVE)

<WANT-TO-TAKE !X>
... <ON !X !Y>...
::)(/FORGET/)
   (/DELETE/ (ON !X !Y))
   (ANSWER I TAKE !X IN MY HAND)
   (/UPDATE/ (EYE !X))
   (/ADD/ (HAND !X))

<WANT-TO-LAY !X !X>
......
::)(/FORGET/)
   (/UPDATE/ (EYE !X))
   (ANSWER YOU ARE FOOLISH $!)

<WANT-TO-LAY !X !Y>
... <ON !X !Y>...
::)(ANSWER BUT !X IS ALREADY ON !Y)
   (/FORGET/)

<WANT-TO-LAY !X FLOOR>
... <HAND !X>...
::)(/FORGET/)
   (/UPDATE/ (EYE !X))
   (/DELETE/ (HAND !X))
   (/ADD/ (ON !X FLOOR))
   (ANSWER I LAY !X ON THE FLOOR)

<WANT-TO-LAY !X !Y>
... <HAND !X> <ON !Z !Y>...
::)(/ADD/ (WANT-TO-LAY !Z FLOOR))
   (ANSWER I MUST FREE !Y OF !Z)

<WANT-TO-LAY !X !Y>
... <HAND !X>...
::)(/FORGET/)
   (/UPDATE/ (EYE !X))
   (/DELETE/ (HAND !X))
   (/ADD/ (ON !X !Y))
   (ANSWER I PUT !X ON !Y)

<WANT-TO-LAY !X !Y>
... <HAND !Z>...
::)(/ADD/ (WANT-TO-LAY !Z FLOOR))
   (ANSWER I LAY !Z WHICH BOTHERS ME)

<WANT-TO-LAY !X !Y>
......
::)(ANSWER WAIT I MUST TAKE IN MY HAND !X)
   (/ADD/ (WANT-TO-TAKE !X))
```

```
<WANT-TO-SEE !X>
. . . . . .
=>(/UPDATE/ (EYE !X))
  (/FORGET/)
  (ANSWER I LOOK AT !X)
```

10.8 Conclusions

We have just discussed the entire robot. You will notice that the central part of the code is only about one hundred lines long (not even completely full), which is ridiculously small for a program that deals with reasoning and natural language. A similar program in BASIC would be a lot bigger. We can compare these one hundred lines to the one hundred and fifty or so that are required in order to write the rules of the universe. The reader can thus appreciate the mass of pragmatic knowledge to which a computing process must have access in order to 'live' in even a simple universe.

The user can easily broaden the scope of the robot by adding new action or state clauses along with their associated rules. As an example, he could give the robot several other hands, rollers on which to move about, or even a companion. He could add complex objects to the universe, requiring two hands to be lifted, or he could introduce restrictions on building piles of objects (such as no sphere to be put on top of a pyramid!).

11 Epilogue

Now that we have reached the end of the book, you have acquired a great quantity of information. Perhaps you consider this to be encyclopaedic, but in fact it represents only some of the numerous facilities made available by LISP. You must set up your own real LISP system: and here you are in for a surprise! You will find differences between this book and your system:

(1) functions with the same name but which give different results (EQ on numbers, etc.)

(2) functions with different names, but with similar results (FUNCTIONP, etc.)

(3) functions whose arguments are not in the same order as here (PUT, GET, MAPCAR, etc.) or functions that have extra arguments specifying additional choices (PRINT, TERPRI, etc.)

(4) other specific functions (or conventions) — CLOCK, LOC, etc., new interactive functions, trace functions and error recovery functions

(5) functions that will have disappeared (MLAMBDA and FLAMBDA which were introduced here for the sake of completeness and because we were explicitly concerned with distinguishing between lists and functions, which certain systems do not do†).

Once your initial surprise has disappeared, we hope that the subject matter in this book will have suitably prepared you for the varied use to be made of

---

†In recent systems, identifiers have often had a double value: the first (which can only be a function created by DE, DF or DM) when the atom is in the functional position, and a second 'normal' one (in other words, one created either by SET or by the application of a function of type EXPR, FEXPR or MEXPR, where it appeared in the parameter list). Usually an atom represents a global function, but if we wish to see the normal value applied, then we replace

    (*atom arguments*. . .)

by

    ((EVAL *atom*) *arguments*. . .)

or we write

    (FUNCALL *atom arguments*. . .)

with

    (DM FUNCALL(FORM)
      (CONS (LIST 'EVAL (CADR FORM))
        (CDDR FORM)))

We use this conversion in uncertain cases as in the problem of SELF in the definition of LET in chapter 10, section 10.2.

LISP, and you will not find it difficult to read and digest various user-manuals.

To the best of my knowledge, no interpreter on the market is the same as the one suggested in this book, which incorporates a little of everything that exists, and which represents a kind of 'middle point'. Although lacking in basic functions (but we have seen how to remedy this), it is relatively rich in function types. The code for this interpreter is given in the Appendix; the understanding of the interpreter contributes a great deal to the understanding of this book and vice versa.

Many LISP dialects co-exist and all contain their own particular constructions (for example, DO in MACLISP, SELF in VLISP, etc.). It is always possible to write constructions particular to one dialect in another one, but this generally tends to lead to reduced performance. The interpreter given in the Appendix may of course be written in these dialects, but would probably not be very fast.

A large number of the tools (and others not even mentioned here) suggested in the exercises are available on LISP systems. One of LISP's important characteristics is the creation of a community that is inclined to introspection. This community mainly studies the art of programming and analyses itself analysing this art. From this we now have some remarkable tools (PHENARETE, CAN, DWIM etc. — see the entries under H. Wertz, D. Goossens and W. Teitelman in the Bibliography in chapter 14) which enrich the environment of the LISP programmer to a great extent. The functions BUILD, CONSTRUCT, MICRO-MATCH, etc. are given as modest examples in this book.

The tools and new programming techniques that they promote stem from the more general concept of Artificial Intelligence and go beyond the aims of this book.

We conclude this book by expressing our wish to see the use of LISP becoming more popular, and by hoping we have aroused your desire to discover, in greater detail, this fantastic means of expression — LISP.

12 Solutions to the Suggested Exercises

1.5.1

ATOM is an atom and therefore an expression

(LIS)P is a badly formed expression (comprising a list followed by an atom)

(L(I(S(P))))) is a badly formed expression (comprising a list followed by a
closing bracket)

(CAR(L I S P)) is a list and even a program if L is a function

(CONS 'CAR "T) is a list and a program whose value is (CAR QUOTE T)

1.5.2

(CAR '(NIL)) has the value NIL

(CDR '(ONE 2 III)) has the value (2 III)

(CADR (CONS 'L '(I S P))) has the value I

(EQ 'T (ATOM 'NIL)) has the value T

(NULL (NULL (ATOM '(NIL)))) has the value NIL

2.1.1

(FACT (FACT 2)) has the same value as

(FACT 2); that is, 2

(FACT −1) leads to an infinite calculation since

(FACT −1) is (* −1 (FACT −2)) which itself requires the calculation of

(FACT −3) which itself requires. . .

2.1.2

Even with this definition, the value of (FACT 3) is 6. The only difference is in
the order of the terms to be multiplied.

The value of (FACT 3) is

(* (FACT 2) N) in the environment where the value of N is 3.

In other words

(* (IF (EQN N 1) 1 (* (FACT (−N 1)) N)) N)

an expression in which the value of N is 3 except in the underlined part where
N will be taken as equal to 2; that is

(*(*(IF (EQN N 1)

 1

 (* (FACT (− N 1)) N))

 N)

 N)

where the value of N is 3, the value of N underlined with a broken line is 2 and the value of N in the expressions underlined with a continuous line is 1. Which leads us to evaluate

(*(* 1 N) N)

where the value of N is 3 except in the underlined part where the value of N is 2; that is
(* 2 N) with the value of N as 3.
In other words, 6.

In this example we see that LISP remembers the environments and is able to restore them.

2.1.3
When applied to a list, the value of UNKNOWN is the left-most atom in this list. So, the value of

(UNKNOWN '(((ATOM AND OTHER
          THINGS)
             WITHOUT)
             ANY IMPORTANCE))

is the atom ATOM.

3.2.1
(EQ (CONS (CAR '(LIST))
          (CDR '(LIST)))

'(LIST)) enables the comparison of two similar lists, but EQ can only return something other than NIL if we provide it with atoms. Consequently the value is NIL.

The value of (CDR (CONS CONS '('LIST NIL))) is ('LIST NIL). The list created by CONS is unprintable since its first term is the function *CONS*. Even though it is unprintable, this does not prevent it from being able to be broken down by CDR.

The value of (EVAL (CONS CONS '('LIST NIL))) is (LIST). Remember that the value of a function is itself! And therefore

(*CONS* 'LIST NIL) has the value (LIST)

3.2.2
The function SPRING-WATER is similar to the function NOT (which is equal to NULL). We can check that

?(SPRING-WATER NIL)
    T
?(SPRING-WATER T)
    NIL

The way in which the function SPRING-WATER has been written is not very

efficient, as the value returned by (NULL EXP) is the same as that returned by
the IF form. Compare with the shortened definition of NOT.

3.2.3

```
(DE TYPE (EXP)
   (IF (ATOM EXP)
       'ATOM
       'LIST ) )
```

3.2.4

We suggest two solutions. The first one uses an extra atom called PROG, which
contains the program to evaluate:

```
(DE TEST ()
   (IF (NULL PROGS)
       'END-OF-TESTS
       (SET 'PROG (CAR PROGS))
       (SET 'PROGS (CDR PROGS))
       (EVAL PROG) ) )
```

The second solution requires an extra function:

```
(DE PROG1 (X Y)
    X )
```

PROG1 returns its first argument as value (but has forced the evaluation of
the second):

```
(DE TEST ()
   (IF (NULL PROGS)
       'END-OF-TESTS
       (PROG1 (EVAL (CAR PROGS))
              (SET 'PROGS
                   (CDR PROGS) ) ) ) )
```

As an example of the use of this function, let us test the programs of
exercise 3.2.1:

```
?(SET 'PROGS '(
?  (EQ (CONS (CAR '(LIST))
?                 (CDR '(LIST)) )
?      '(LIST) )
?  (CDR (CONS CONS '('LIST NIL)))
?  (EVAL (CONS CONS '('LIST NIL))) ))
```

Once these programs are arranged in a list as the value of the atom PROGS,
we just need to call the function TEST:

```
?(TEST)
   NIL
?(TEST)
   ('LIST NIL)
?(TEST)
   (LIST)
?(TEST)
   END-OF-TESTS
?(TEST)
   END-OF-TESTS
```

3.4.1

$\dfrac{1 + \sqrt{5}}{2}$ is written as

```
(/ (+ 1 (SQRT 5)) 2)
```

$\dfrac{x^n}{n!}$ is written as

```
(/ (EXP X N) (FACT N))
```

3.4.2

By the first method, $\binom{n}{p}$ is written as:

```
(DE C (N P)
  (/ (FACT N)
     (* (FACT P) (FACT (- N P))) ) )
```

As this way of programming is very inefficient, we can use the second relations to write:

```
(DE C (N P)
  (IF (OR (EQ P 0)
          (EQ P N) )
      1
      (+ (C (- N 1) P)
         (C (- N 1) (- P 1)) ) ) )
```

3.4.3

```
(DE SEQUENCE (ONE)
   (IF (EQ ONE 1) NIL
       (CONS ONE
             (SEQUENCE (IF (ZEROP (MOD ONE 2))
                           (/ ONE 2)
                           (ADD1 (* 3 ONE)) )) )) )
```

3.6.1

```
?(PRINT (+ 2 3))
5
    5

?(PRINT '(+ 2 3))
(+ 2 3)
    (+ 2 3)

?(PRINT (CONS (READ) (READ)))A(B)
(A B)
    (A B)
```

3.6.2

```
(DE LPRINT (EXP)
  (IF (CONSP EXP)
      (PROGN (PRINT (CAR EXP))
             (LPRINT (CDR EXP)) ) ) )
```

3.8.1

```
(DM WHILE (CALL)
  (LIST 'IF
        (CADR CALL)
        (LIST 'PROGN
              (CONS 'PROGN
                    (CDDR CALL) )
              CALL ) ) )
```

The form equivalent to (WHILE *condition expressions*. . .) is

(IF *condition* (PROGN (PROGN *expressions*. . .)
                (WHILE *condition expressions*. . .)))

Programming a macro-function is much better than programming an FEXPR as there are no restrictions on the arguments *condition* and *expressions*. . . In fact, no variable is masked by the WHILE loop, which is not the case when programming an FEXPR. The suggested example is an infinite loop as the value of the identifier CONDITION, which appears in the WHILE loop, will be itself (because of WHILE1) and as the loop condition will always be True, there will be a never-ending print of AGAIN, AGAIN, AGAIN, . . .

3.8.2

```
(DM FLAMBDA (CALL)
  (LIST 'MLAMBDA
        (CADR CALL)
        (LIST 'SET
              (LIST 'QUOTE
                    (CAADR CALL) )
              (LIST 'CDR
                    (CAADR CALL) ) )
        (LIST 'LIST
              ''QUOTE
              (CONS 'PROGN
                    (CDDR CALL) ) ) ) )
```

This program corresponds to the following. Each time we have to evaluate

  ((FLAMBDA (*variable*) *expressions*. . .) *arguments*. . .)

we will, in fact, evaluate the equivalent form

  ((MLAMBDA (*variable*) (SET '*variable* (CDR *variable*))
                    (LIST 'QUOTE (PROGN *expressions*. . .)))
  arguments. . .)

In chapter 6 we will meet a more convenient way to generate lists (by using the function BUILD) in comparison with these inextricable muddles of CONS, LIST and QUOTE!

3.8.3

```
(DE SIGNATURE (EXP)
  (IF (ATOM EXP)
      (IF (NUMBERP EXP) 'NUMBERP
          (IF (SYMBOLP EXP) 'SYMBOLP
                            'FUNCTIONP ) )
      (MAPCAR EXP SIGNATURE) ) )
```

3.8.4
We give two solutions. The first one is very simple (especially as the predicate EQUAL exists on all interpreters).

```
(DE TEST-SIGNATURE (S E)
  (EQUAL S (SIGNATURE E)) )
```

The second solution allows all the signature discrepancies to be listed:

```
(DE TEST-SIGNATURE (S E)
  (IF (AND (ATOM E)(ATOM S))
      (IF ((EVAL S) E)
          T
          (PRINT (LIST 'NOT
                        (LIST S E) ))
          NIL )
      (IF (AND (CONSP E)(CONSP S))
          (IF (TEST-SIGNATURE (CAR S) (CAR E))
              (TEST-SIGNATURE (CDR S) (CDR E))
              (TEST-SIGNATURE (CDR S) (CDR E))
              NIL )
          (PRINT (LIST 'INCOMPATIBLE S E))
          NIL ) ) )
```

By evaluating

```
?(TEST-SIGNATURE '(NUMBERP
?                  SYMBOLP
?                  SYMBOLP
?                  (NUMBERP SYMBOLP)
?                  SYMBOLP )
?                  '(3 A 2 (S A B)) )
```

we will get

```
(NOT (SYMBOLP 2))
(NOT (NUMBERP S))
(INCOMPATIBLE NIL (B))
(INCOMPATIBLE (SYMBOLP) NIL)
   NIL
```

You will notice the predicate names in the signature, which are used to test the corresponding term.

The predicates AND and EQUAL will be explained in chapter 5 and exercise 3.8.5 (below) respectively.

3.8.5

```
(DE EQUAL (L1 L2)
  (OR (EQ L1 L2)
      (AND (CONSP L1)
           (CONSP L2)
           (EQUAL (CAR L1)(CAR L2))
           (EQUAL (CDR L1)(CDR L2)) ) ) )
```

4.1.1

```
(DE MIRROR (L)
  (IF (CONSP L)
      (APPEND (MIRROR (CDR L))
              (LIST (MIRROR (CAR L))) )
      L ) )
```

4.1.2

```
(DE EGYPT (P Q)
  (IF (ZEROP P) NIL
      (LET ((N (LET ((MU (LAMBDA(I)
                     (IF (GE (* P I) Q)
                         I
                         (MU (ADD1 I)) ) )))
                  (MU 1) )))
           (CONS N
                 (EGYPT (- (* P N) Q)
                        (* Q N) ) ) ) ) )
```

The function MU calculates the first integer number (i) which satisfies the condition:

$$p * (i + 1) \geqslant q$$

or in other words

$$\frac{p}{q} \geqslant \frac{1}{i + 1}$$

The function MU is local and will disappear when all the calculations have been done. When the integer number has been found, it becomes the local value of N and the process continues recursively with the fraction

$$\frac{p}{q} - \frac{1}{n}$$

4.1.3

```
(DE MEMBER (A L)
 (AND (CONSP L)
      (OR (EQ A (CAR L))
          (MEMBER A (CDR L)) ) ) )
```

5.1.1

ATOMS is easily defined along the same lines as the version of FLAT which uses buffer variables:

```
(DE ATOMS (L)
  (ATOMS1 L NIL) )

(DE ATOMS1 (L R)
  (IF (ATOM L)
      (IF (OR (NULL L)
              (MEMBER L R) )
          R
          (CONS L R) )
      (ATOMS1 (CAR L)
              (ATOMS1 (CDR L) R) ) ) )
```

5.1.2

```
(DE FACT (N)
  (FACT1 N 1) )


(DE FACT1 (N R)
  (IF (LE N 1)
      R
      (FACT1 (SUB1 N) (* N R)) ) )
```

5.1.3

```
(DM IF (CALL)
  (LIST 'COND
        (LIST (CADR CALL)(CADDR CALL))
        (CONS 'T (CONS NIL (CDDDR CALL))) ) )
```

5.1.4
We just need to alter the function NEIGHBOURS:

```
(DE NEIGHBOURS (PLACE)
  (APPEND (CDR (ASSOC PLACE
                      (CDR LABYRINTH) ))
          (MAPCAN LABYRINTH
                  (LAMBDA(L)
            (IF (MEMBER PLACE (CDR L))
                (LIST L) ) ) ) ) )
```

6.1.1

```
(DM UNTIL (CALL)
  (BUILD '((LAMBDA()
            (IF (:= (CADR CALL))
                NIL
                (:= CALL) ) )
          (:↑ (CDDR CALL)) ))  )
(DM NLAMBDA (CALL)
  (BUILD '(MLAMBDA (CALL)
    (LIST (LAMBDA (:↑ (CDR CALL)))
          (CONS 'LIST (CDR CALL)) ) )) )
```

6.1.2

CONSTRUCT is written along the same lines as BUILD:

```
; VI.1.2
(DE CONSTRUCT (L)
  (IF (CONSP L)
      (IF (CONSP (CAR L))
          (LET ((FN (GET 'CONSTRUCT (CAAR L))))
               (IF FN (FN L)
                   (LIST 'CONS
                         (CONSTRUCT (CAR L))
                         (CONSTRUCT (CDR L)) ) ) )
          (LIST 'CONS (LIST 'QUOTE (CAR L))
                      (CONSTRUCT (CDR L)) ) )
      (LIST 'QUOTE L) ) )
```

Note that this is an approximate program, and that certain improvements would need to be done; for example

```
?(CONSTRUCT '(IF T CAR CDR))
   (CONS (QUOTE IF) (CONS (QUOTE T) (CONS (QUOTE CAR) (CONS
(QUOTE CDR) (QUOTE NIL)))))
```

could be simplified as, with regard to BUILD, it is a constant:

```
(QUOTE (IF T CAR CDR))
```

The properties associated with CONSTRUCT are

```
(PUT 'CONSTRUCT ':= (LAMBDA(L)
  (LIST 'CONS (CADAR L)
              (CONSTRUCT (CDR L)) ) ))
```

```
(PUT 'CONSTRUCT ':↑ (LAMBDA(L)
  (LIST 'APPEND (CADAR L)
                (CONSTRUCT (CDR L)) ) ))
```

7.1.1

```
(DE SUBST (X Y Z)
 (IF (CONSP Z)
     (CONS (SUBST X Y (CAR Z))
           (SUBST X Y (CDR Z)) )
     (IF (EQ Y Z) X Z) ) )
```

```
(DE LENGTH (L)
  (IF (CONSP L)
      (ADD1 (LENGTH (CDR L)))
      0 ) )
```

7.1.2

```
(DE COUNT (L)
  (SWEEP L
         PLUS
         (LAMBDA(A)(IF A 1 0)) ) )
```

7.1.3

```
(DE LIT (L END FN)
  (IF (CONSP L)
      (FN (CAR L)
          (LIT (CDR L) END FN) )
      END ) )
```

7.1.4

```
(DE DELETE (A L)
  (LIT L NIL
    (LAMBDA(X R)
           (IF (EQ X A) R
               (CONS X R) ) ) ) )
```

8.1.1

```
(DE REVERSE (L)
  (REVERSE1 L NIL) )

(DE REVERSE1 (L P)
  (IF (CONSP L)
      (REVERSE1 (CDR L) (RPLACD L P))
      P ) )
```

This variation returns a list as follows:

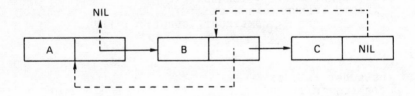

9.1.1

```
(DE LPRINT (L)
  (IF (CONSP L)
      (PROGN (PRIN1 (CAR L))
             (PRIN1 '$ )
             (LPRINT (CDR L)) ) )
    L )
```

9.1.2

```
(DM ADVISE (CALL)
  (LET ((D (FUNCTIONP (EVAL (CADR CALL)))))
     (IF (AND D
              (CONSP D)
              (EQ (CAR D) 'LAMBDA) )
         (BUILD !
  (DE (:= (CADR CALL))
      (:= (CADR D))
      (LET ((BEFORE (:= (CADDR CALL)))
            (RESULT (PROGN (:↑ (CDDR D))))
            (AFTER (:= (CADDDR CALL))) )
         RESULT ) ) ) ) ) )
```

13 Appendix: LISP in LISP

```
; *********** P R I N T   P A C K A G E ****************************************

(DE %PRINT (EXP)
  (%PRIN1-EXP EXP)        ; print argument and call terpri
  (TERPRI)
  EXP )

(DE %PRIN1-EXP (EXP)    ; print only one expression
  (IF (%ATOM EXP)         ; according to its type
      (IF (%FUNCTIONP EXP)
          (PROGN (TERPRI)          ; special case of functions
                 (PRINT MSG7) )
          (PRIN1 EXP) )
      (PRIN1 '$()
      (%PRIN1-EXPS EXP) ) )

(DE %PRIN1-EXPS (EXPS) ; print a sequence of expressions
  (IF (NULL EXPS)          ; with appropriate separators
      (PRIN1 '$))
      (IF (%ATOM EXPS)
          (PROGN (PRIN1 '$.$ )          ; last cdr not nil
                 (%PRIN1-EXP EXPS)
                 (PRIN1 '$)) )
          (%PRIN1-EXP (%CAR EXPS))
          (IF (NULL (%CDR EXPS)) NIL (PRIN1 '$ ))
          (%PRIN1-EXPS (%CDR EXPS)) ) ) )


(DE %TOPLEVEL ()           ; toplevel loop
  (PRINT 'LISP$ IS$ WINNING$ AGAIN)
  (LET ((RESULT (%EVAL (%READ)) INITIAL-ENV)))
       (TERPRI)
       (PRIN1 '$ $ $ ) ; 3 blanks lead results
       (%PRINT RESULT) )
  (%TOPLEVEL) )            ; ad vitam aeternam


; ********************** E V A L U A T I O N ********************

(DE %EVAL (EXP ENV)
  (COND ((NUMBERP EXP) EXP)
        ((SYMBOLP  EXP)
         (LET ((V (%VALUE EXP ENV)))    ; if unbound ask for a value
              (IF (%UNKNOWNP V)
                  (PROGN (PRIN1 MSG1)(%PRINT EXP)
                         (%PRINT MSG2)
                         (%EVAL (%READ) ENV) )
                  V ) ) )
        ((%FUNCTIONP EXP) EXP)
        ((%CONSP EXP)  ; form evaluation
         (LET ((V (%APPLY (%EVAL (%CAR EXP)
                                 ENV) ; if incorrect ask for a value
                          EXP
                          ENV
                          ENV )))
```

144

```
            (IF (%UNKNOWNP V)
                (PROGN (PRIN1 MSG5)(%PRINT EXP)
                       (%PRINT MSG6)
                       (%EVAL (%READ) ENV) )
                V ) ) )
         (T (%ERROR)) ) )            ; useless but ...

(DE %APPLY (FN FORM ENVARGS ENVBODY)      ; invocation of function
   (COND ((%FUNCTIONP FN)                 ; according to its type
         (LET ((TYPE (%FUNCTION-TYPE FN)))
             (COND ((EQ TYPE 'SUBR)
                    (%EXECUTE (%FUNCTION-NAME FN)
                              (%EVLIS (%CDR FORM) ENVARGS)
                              ENVBODY ) )
                   ((EQ TYPE 'FSUBR)
                    ( %EXECUTE (%FUNCTION-NAME FN)
                               FORM
                               ENVBODY ) )
                   ((EQ TYPE 'EXPR)
                    (%EPROGN (%BODY-FIELD FN)
                             %UNKNOWN
                             (BIND
                               (SPREAD (%ARGS-FIELD FN)
                                       (%EVLIS (%CDR FORM)
                                               ENVARGS ) )
                               ENVBODY ) ) )
                   ((EQ TYPE 'NEXPR)
                    (%EPROGN (%BODY-FIELD FN)
                             %UNKNOWN
                             (BIND
                               (SPREAD (%ARGS-FIELD FN)
                                       (LIST (%EVLIS (%CDR FORM)

                                                     ENVARGS )) )
                               ENVBODY ) ) )
                   ((EQ TYPE 'FEXPR)
                    (%EPROGN (%BODY-FIELD FN)
                             %UNKNOWN
                             (BIND (SPREAD (%ARGS-FIELD FN)
                                           (LIST (%CDR FORM)) )
                                   ENVBODY ) ) )
                   ((EQ TYPE 'MEXPR)
                    (%EVAL (%EPROGN (%BODY-FIELD FN)
                                    %UNKNOWN
                                    (BIND
                                      (SPREAD (%ARGS-FIELD FN)
                                              (LIST FORM) )
                                      ENVBODY ) )
                           ENVARGS ) )
                   ((EQ TYPE 'CLOSURE)        ; the famous funarg
                    (%APPLY (%FUNCTION-FIELD FN)
                            FORM
                            ENVARGS
                            (%ENV-FIELD FN) ) )
                   ((EQ TYPE 'DELAY)          ; for lazy purposes
                    (%EPROGN (%BODY-FIELD FN)
                             %UNKNOWN
                             (BIND
                               (SPREAD (%ARGS-FIELD FN)
                                       (%CLOSLIS (%CDR FORM)
                                                 ENVARGS ) )
                               ENVBODY ) ) )
                   (T (%ERROR)) ) ) )
         (T (PRIN1 MSG3)(%PRINT FN)           ; first term must be a function
            (%PRINT MSG4)                     ; if not ask for one
            (%APPLY (%EVAL (%READ) ENVARGS)
```

```
                                FORM
                                ENVARGS
                                ENVBODY ) ) ) )
```

; ************** E R R O R   M E S S A G E S **************

; ERROR if *****message
; WARNING if ***message

```
(CSET 'MSG1 '*****UNBOUND-ATOM:)
(CSET 'MSG2 '***ATOM-VALUE?)
(CSET 'MSG3 '*****FIRST-TERM-IS-NOT-A-FUNCTION:)
(CSET 'MSG4 '***FUNCTION-VALUE?)
(CSET 'MSG5 '*****ERRONEOUS-FORM:)
(CSET 'MSG6 '***FORM-VALUE?)
(CSET 'MSG7 '***NOT-PRINTABLE)
(CSET 'MSG8 '*****WRONG-ARGUMENTS-NUMBER:)
(CSET 'MSG9 '*****ERRONEOUS-VARIABLE:)
(CSET 'MSG10 '***IGNORED-BINDING)
(CSET 'MSG11 '*****FIRST-ARGUMENT-IS-NOT-A-SYMBOL:)
```

; ************* M A P P E R S **********************************

```
(DE %OR (FORMS ENV)              ; boolean or
  (IF (%CONSP FORMS)
      (OR (%EVAL (%CAR FORMS) ENV)
          (%OR (%CDR FORMS) ENV) )
      NIL ) )

(DE %AND (FORMS ENV)             ; boolean and
  (IF (%CONSP FORMS)
      (AND (%EVAL (%CAR FORMS) ENV)
           (%AND (%CDR FORMS) ENV) )
      T ) )

(DE %EPROGN (FORMS PREVIOUS ENV) ; sequential evaluation of forms
  (IF (NULL FORMS)
      PREVIOUS
      (%EPROGN (%CDR FORMS)
               (%EVAL (%CAR FORMS) ENV)
               ENV ) ) )

(DE %EVLIS (FORMS ENV)                ; map %eval on forms
  (IF (NULL FORMS)  NIL
      (CONS (%EVAL (%CAR FORMS) ENV)
            (%EVLIS (%CDR FORMS) ENV) ) ) )

(DE %CLOSLIS (FORMS ENV)            ; map %closure on forms
  (IF (NULL FORMS)  NIL
      (CONS (MK-CLOSURE (%CAR FORMS) ENV)
            (%CLOSLIS (%CDR FORMS) ENV) ) ) )
```

; *************** E N V I R O N M E N T   H A N D L E R **********

```
; environment are a lists
(DE %SET (A V)
  (IF (SYMBOLP A)
      (CDR (%CHANGE-VALUE A V ENV))
      (PRIN1 MSG11)(%PRINT A)
      (%PRINT MSG2)
      (%SET (%EVAL (%READ) ENV) V) ) ) ; ask for a symbol

(CSETQ BIND NCONC)

(DE %VALUE (A ENV)               ; get value of symbol a in env
   (%VALUE1 ( ASSOC A ENV)) )
```

```
(DE %VALUE1 (R)
    (IF (NULL R)
        %UNKNOWN
        (%CDR R) ) )

(DE SPREAD (LV LA)                   ; spread args upon vars
   (COND ((NULL LV) NIL)
         ((SYMBOLP LV)(CONS (CONS LV LA) NIL))
         ((AND (%CONSP LV) (SYMBOLP (%CAR LV)))
          (IF (%CONSP LA)
              (CONS (CONS (%CAR LV) (%CAR LA))
                    (SPREAD (%CDR LV) (%CDR LA)) )
              (CONS (CONS (%CAR LV) LA)
                    (SPREAD (%CDR LV) NIL) ) ) )
         ((%CONSP LV)(PRIN1 MSG9)(%PRINT (%CAR LV))
                     (%PRINT MSG10)
                     (SPREAD (%CDR LV)
                             (IF (%CONSP LA) (%CDR LA)) ) )
         (T (PRIN1 MSG9)(%PRINT LV)
            (%PRINT MSG10)
            NIL ) ) )

(DE %CHANGE-VALUE (A V ENV)          ; modify environment such that
   (COND                             ; value of a is v
        ((%EQ A (%CAR (%CAR ENV)))
         (RPLACD (%CAR ENV) V) )
        ((NULL (%CDR ENV))
         (CADR (RPLACD ENV (LIST (CONS A V)))) )
        (T (%CHANGE-VALUE A V (%CDR ENV))) ) )

; *********** E X E C U T I O N ****************************

(DE %EXECUTE (AFN ARGS ENV)          ; launch subr and fsubr
   (LET ((F (GET '%EXECUTE AFN)))
        (IF F (IF (GE (LENGTH ARGS) (CAR F))
                  (EVAL (CDR F))
                  (PRIN1 MSG8)(%PRINT  FORM)
                  (%PRINT MSG6)
                  (%EVAL (%READ) ENV) )
              (%ERROR) ) ) )

; **************** P R E D I C A T E s *********************

; three logical values : TRUE, FALSE, UNDEFINED

(DE %NOT (E)
   (IF (%UNKNOWNP E) %UNKNOWN
       (NOT E) ) )

(DE %UNKNOWNP (EXP)
   (EQ EXP '%UNKNOWN) )

(DE %FUNCTIONP (EXP)
   (IF (AND (CONSP EXP)
            (EQ (CAR EXP) %%FM) )
       (IF (MEMBER (CADR EXP) '(SUBR FSUBR))
           T
           (%DEFINITION EXP) ) ) )

(DE %CONSP (EXP)
   (AND (CONSP EXP)
        (NOT (EQ (CAR EXP) %%FM)) ) )

(DE %ATOM (EXP)
   (NOT (%CONSP EXP)) )
```

```
(DE %EQ (EXP1 EXP2)        ; %eq works on numbers
  (OR (AND (NUMBERP EXP1)
           (NUMBERP EXP2)
           (EQUAL EXP1 EXP2) )
      (EQ EXP1 EXP2) ) )
```

```
; **************** L I S T   S E L E C T O R S ****************************
```

```
(DE %CAR (EXP)
  (IF (%CONSP EXP) (CAR EXP) %UNKNOWN) )
```

```
(DE %CDR (EXP)
  (IF (%CONSP EXP) (CDR EXP) %UNKNOWN) )
```

```
(DE %CADR (EXP)
  (%CAR (%CDR EXP)) )
```

```
; ************** A R G U M E N T   S E L E C T O R S *************
```

```
(DE %ARG1 (ARGS)
  (IF (%CONSP ARGS)
      (%CAR ARGS) ) )
```

```
(DE %ARG2 (ARGS)
  (IF (%CONSP ARGS)
      (%ARG1 (%CDR ARGS)) ) )
```

```
(DE %ARG3 (ARGS)
  (IF (%CONSP ARGS)
      (%ARG2 (%CDR ARGS)) ) )
```

```
(DE %ARGS2-AND-OTHERS (ARGS)
  (IF (%CONSP ARGS)
      (%CDR ARGS) ) )
```

```
(DE %ARGS3-AND-OTHERS (ARGS)
  (IF (%CONSP ARGS)
      (%ARGS2-AND-OTHERS (%CDR ARGS)) ) )
```

```
(DE %ARGS4-AND-OTHERS (ARGS)
  (IF (%CONSP ARGS)
      (%ARGS3-AND-OTHERS (%CDR ARGS)) ) )
```

```
; ************** A R I T H M E T I C ****************************
```

```
(DE %PLUS (N P)
  (IF (AND (NUMBERP N)(NUMBERP P))
      (PLUS N P)
      %UNKNOWN ) )
```

```
(DE %TIMES (N P)
  (IF (AND (NUMBERP N)(NUMBERP P))
      (TIMES N P)
      %UNKNOWN ) )
```

```
(DE %DIFFERENCE (N P)
  (IF (AND (NUMBERP N)(NUMBERP P))
      (DIFFERENCE N P)
      %UNKNOWN ) )
```

```
(DE %QUOTIENT (N P)
  (IF (AND (NUMBERP N)(NUMBERP P))
      (QUOTIENT N P)
      %UNKNOWN ) )
```

```
(DE %REMAINDER (N P)
  (IF (AND (NUMBERP N)(NUMBERP P))
      (REMAINDER N P)
      %UNKNOWN ) )

(DE %GREATERP (N P)
  (IF (AND (NUMBERP N)(NUMBERP P))
      (GREATERP N P)
      %UNKNOWN ) )

(DE %LESSP (N P)
  (IF (AND (NUMBERP N)(NUMBERP P))
      (LESSP N P)
      %UNKNOWN ) )

; **************** F U N C T I O N  S E L E C T O R S ************

(DE %DEFINITION (FN)     ; return a form whose value is fn
      (CONS (LET ((TYPE (CADR FN)))
                 (COND ((EQ TYPE 'EXPR)     'LAMBDA)
                       ((EQ TYPE 'FEXPR) 'FLAMBDA)
                       ((EQ TYPE 'NEXPR) 'NLAMBDA)
                       ((EQ TYPE 'MEXPR) 'MLAMBDA)
                       ((EQ TYPE 'DELAY) 'DLAMBDA)
                       ((EQ TYPE 'CLOSURE) 'CLAMBDA) ) )
            (IF (EQ 'CLOSURE (CADR FN))
                (LIST (%DEFINITION (CADDR FN))
                      (CDDDR FN) )
                (CONS (CADDR FN)
                      (CDDDR FN) ) ) ) )

(DE %ARGS-FIELD (FN)
  (IF (AND (%FUNCTIONP FN)
           (NOT (EQ (%FUNCTION-TYPE FN) 'CLOSURE)))
      (CADDR FN) ) )

(DE %BODY-FIELD (FN)
  (IF (AND (%FUNCTIONP FN)
           (NOT (EQ (%FUNCTION-TYPE FN) 'CLOSURE)) )
      (CDDDR FN) ) )

(DE %FUNCTION-TYPE (FN)
  (IF (%FUNCTIONP FN)
      (CADR FN) ) )
(DE %FUNCTION-FIELD (FN)
  (IF (AND (%FUNCTIONP FN)
           (EQ (%FUNCTION-TYPE FN) 'CLOSURE) )
      (CADDR FN) ) )

(DE %ENV-FIELD (FN)
  (IF (AND (%FUNCTIONP FN)
           (EQ (%FUNCTION-TYPE FN) 'CLOSURE) )
      (CDDDR FN) ) )

(DE %FUNCTION-NAME (FN)
  (IF (AND (%FUNCTIONP FN)
           (OR (EQ (CADR FN) 'SUBR)
               (EQ (CADR FN) 'FSUBR) ) )
      (CDDR FN)
      (%ERROR) ) )


; *************** F U N C T I O N  C O N S T R U C T O R S *******************

(DE MK-CLOSURE (FN ENV)
  (CONS %%FM (CONS 'CLOSURE (CONS FN ENV))) )
```

```
(DE MK-FSUBR (NAME)
  (CONS %%FM (CONS 'FSUBR NAME)) )

(DE MK-SUBR (NAME)
  (CONS %%FM (CONS 'SUBR NAME)) )


(DE MK-FUNCTION (TYPE ARGS BODY)
  (CONS %%FM (CONS TYPE (CONS ARGS BODY))) )

; ********* I M P L E M E N T A T I O N   C O N S T A N T S ******************

(CSET '%%FM '%%%%)                  ; functional marker

(CSET '%UNKNOWN '%UNKNOWN) ; unknown is really not known !

(CSET 'INITIAL-ENV
      '((NIL . NIL)(T . T)) )

; ******************** P R I M I T I V E S ****************************

(DE PREPARE (EXP)   ; prepare primitives to check their arguments count
  (CONS (COND
          ((OR (APPEAR '%ARGS4-AND-OTHERS EXP)
               (APPEAR '%ARG3 EXP) ) 3 )
          ((OR (APPEAR '%ARGS3-AND-OTHERS EXP)
               (APPEAR '%ARG2 EXP) ) 2 )
          ((OR (APPEAR '%ARGS2-AND-OTHERS EXP)
               (APPEAR '%ARG1 EXP) ) 1 )
          (T 0) )
        EXP ) )

((LAMBDA (PRIMITIVES)            ; load subr codes
   (MAPC PRIMITIVES
         (LAMBDA (PRIMITIVE)
                 (%CHANGE-VALUE (CAR PRIMITIVE)
                               (MK-SUBR (CAR PRIMITIVE))
                               INITIAL-ENV )
                 (PUT '%EXECUTE
                      (CAR PRIMITIVE)
                      (PREPARE (CADR PRIMITIVE)) ) ) ) )
 '(
(CAR (%CAR (%ARG1 ARGS)))
(FIRST (%CAR (%ARG1 ARGS)))
(CADR (%CAR (%CDR (%ARG1 ARGS))))
(CADAR (%CAR (%CDR (%CAR (%ARG1 ARGS)))))
(LIST ARGS)
(CDDR (%CDR (%CDR (%ARG1 ARGS))))
(CDAR (%CDR (%CAR (%ARG1 ARGS))))
(CAAR (%CAR (%CAR (%ARG1 ARGS))))
(CDR (%CDR (%ARG1 ARGS)))
(REST (%CDR (%ARG1 ARGS)))
(CONS (CONS (%ARG1 ARGS) (%ARG2 ARGS)))
(INSERT (CONS (%ARG1 ARGS) (%ARG2 ARGS)))
(EVAL (%EVAL (%ARG1 ARGS) ENV))
(FUNCTION (MK-CLOSURE (%ARG1 ARGS) ENV))
(SET (%SET (%ARG1 ARGS) (%ARG2 ARGS)))
(ATOM (%ATOM (%ARG1 ARGS)) )
(EQ (%EQ (%ARG1 ARGS) (%ARG2 ARGS)) )
(CONSP (%CONSP (%ARG1 ARGS)) )
(GET (GET (%ARG1 ARGS) (%ARG2 ARGS)))
(PUT (PUT (%ARG1 ARGS) (%ARG2 ARGS) (%ARG3 ARGS)))
(REVERSE (%REVERSE (%ARG1 ARGS)))
(APPEND (%APPEND (%ARG1 ARGS) (%ARG2 ARGS)))
(RPLACA (IF (%CONSP (%ARG1 ARGS))
            (RPLACA (%ARG1 ARGS) (%ARG2 ARGS))
            %UNKNOWN ))
```

```
(RPLACD (IF (%CONSP (%ARG1 ARGS))
                (RPLACD (%ARG1 ARGS) (%ARG2 ARGS))
                %UNKNOWN ))
(FUNCTIONP (%FUNCTIONP (%ARG1 ARGS)) )
(NUMBERP (NUMBERP (%ARG1 ARGS)) )
(SYMBOLP (SYMBOLP (%ARG1 ARGS)) )
(STOP (PROGN (%PRINT 'DEBUG-MODE)(TOPLEVEL))) ; to debug interpretor
(NULL (NULL (%ARG1 ARGS)))
(NOT (NOT (%ARG1 ARGS)))
(EQN (%EQ (%ARG1 ARGS) (%ARG2 ARGS)) )
(PLUS (LIT ARGS 0 %PLUS))
(+     (LIT ARGS 0 %PLUS))
(*     (LIT ARGS 1 %TIMES))
(TIMES (LIT ARGS 1 %TIMES))
(DIFFERENCE (%DIFFERENCE (%ARG1 ARGS) (%ARG2 ARGS)))
(- (%DIFFERENCE (%ARG1 ARGS) (%ARG2 ARGS)))
(/ (%QUOTIENT (%ARG1 ARGS) (%ARG2 ARGS)))
(QUOTIENT (%QUOTIENT (%ARG1 ARGS) (%ARG2 ARGS)))
(MOD (%REMAINDER (%ARG1 ARGS) (%ARG2 ARGS)))
(REMAINDER (%REMAINDER (%ARG1 ARGS) (%ARG2 ARGS)))
(PROG1 (%ARG1 ARGS))
(ADD1 (%PLUS (%ARG1 ARGS) 1))
(SUB1 (%DIFFERENCE (%ARG1 ARGS) 1))
(GT (%GREATERP (%ARG1 ARGS) (%ARG2 ARGS)))
(GREATERP (%GREATERP (%ARG1 ARGS) (%ARG2 ARGS)))
(LT (%LESSP (%ARG1 ARGS) (%ARG2 ARGS)))
(LESSP (%LESSP (%ARG1 ARGS) (%ARG2 ARGS)))
(GE (%NOT (%LESSP (%ARG1 ARGS) (%ARG2 ARGS))))
(LE (%NOT (%GREATERP (%ARG1 ARGS) (%ARG2 ARGS))))
(PRINT (%PRINT (%ARG1 ARGS))),
(READ (%READ))
(TOPLEVEL (%TOPLEVEL))
(PRIN1 (%PRIN1-EXF (%ARG1 ARGS)))
(TERPRI (TERPRI))
   ) )


((LAMBDA (PRIMITIVES) ; load fsubr codes
    (MAPC PRIMITIVES
          (LAMBDA (PRIMITIVE)
                 (%CHANGE-VALUE (CAR PRIMITIVE)
                               (MK-FSUBR (CAR PRIMITIVE))
                               INITIAL-ENV )
                 (PUT '%EXECUTE
                      (CAR PRIMITIVE)
                      (PREPARE (CADR PRIMITIVE)) ) ) ) )
 '(
(LAMBDA (MK-FUNCTION 'EXPR (%ARG2 ARGS)
                    (%ARGS3-AND-OTHERS ARGS)))
(NLAMBDA (MK-FUNCTION 'NEXPR (%ARG2 ARGS)
                    (%ARGS3-AND-OTHERS ARGS)))
(FLAMBDA (MK-FUNCTION 'FEXPR (%ARG2 ARGS)
                    (%ARGS3-AND-OTHERS ARGS)))
(MLAMBDA (MK-FUNCTION 'MEXPR (%ARG2 ARGS)
                    (%ARGS3-AND-OTHERS ARGS)))
(DE (PROGN (%SET (%ARG2 ARGS)
                (MK-FUNCTION 'EXPR
                            (%ARG3 ARGS)
                            (%ARGS4-AND-OTHERS ARGS) ) )
          (%ARG2 ARGS) ))
(DN (PROGN (%SET (%ARG2 ARGS)
                (MK-FUNCTION 'NEXPR
                            (%ARG3 ARGS)
                            (%ARGS4-AND-OTHERS ARGS) ) )
          (%ARG2 ARGS) ))
```

```
(DF (PROGN (%SET (%ARG2 ARGS)
                 (MK-FUNCTION 'FEXPR
                              (%ARG3 ARGS)
                              (%ARGS4-AND-OTHERS ARGS) ) )
           (%ARG2 ARGS) ))
(DM (PROGN (%SET (%ARG2 ARGS)
                 (MK-FUNCTION 'MEXPR
                              (%ARG3 ARGS)
                              (%ARGS4-AND-OTHERS ARGS) ) )
           (%ARG2 ARGS) ))
(QUOTE (%ARG2 ARGS))
(OR (%OR (%ARGS2-AND-OTHERS ARGS) ENV))
(AND (%AND (%ARGS2-AND-OTHERS ARGS) ENV))
(LET (%EPROGN (%ARGS3-AND-OTHERS ARGS)
              NIL
              (BIND (SPREAD (MAPCAR (%ARG2 ARGS) %CAR)
                            (%EVLIS (MAPCAR (%ARG2 ARGS) %CADR)
                                    ENV ) )
                    ENV ) ))
(PROGN (%EPROGN (%ARGS2-AND-OTHERS ARGS)
                NIL
                ENV ))
(IF (IF (NULL (%EVAL (%ARG2 ARGS) ENV))
        (%EPROGN (%ARGS4-AND-OTHERS ARGS)
                 NIL
                 ENV )
        (%EVAL (%ARG3 ARGS) ENV) ))
   ))
```

14 Bibliography

The bibliography relating to LISP is enormous, and so only general documents and works or articles quoted in the text are listed here.

Allen, J. R., *Anatomy of LISP*, Computer Science Series, McGraw-Hill, 1978.

Allen, J. R., 'Computing, LISP and you', *Microcomputing*, Feb. 1982, pp. 28-42.

BYTE Special Issue on LISP, March 1979.

Chailloux, J., 'Le LISP 80, le Manuel de Référence', *INRIA*, May 1983.

Chailloux, J., 'LISP: Un langage pas comme les autres', *L'Ordinateur Individuel*, No. 9, July 1979.

Church, A., 'The calculi of lambda-conversion', *Annals of Mathematics Studies*, Princeton University Press, New Jersey, 1941.

Goossens, D., 'Compréhension visuelle de programmes controlée par méta-filtrage', *AFCET-GROPLAN*, Bulletin No. 9, 1979. [CAN]

Greussay, P., 'Aides à la programmation en LISP: Outils d'observation et de compréhension', *AFCET-GROPLAN*, Bulletin No. 9, 1979.

Marti, J., Hearn, A. C., Griss, M. L. and Griss, C., 'Standard LISP Report', *ACM SIGPLAN Notices*, Vol. 14, No. 10, Oct. 1979, pp. 48-68.

McCarthy, J., 'History of LISP', in *History of Programming Languages* (Ed.: R. L. Wexelblat), Academic Press, 1981, pp. 173-197.

McCarthy, J., Abrahams, P. W., Edwards, D. J., Hart, T. P. and Levin, M. I., *LISP 1.5 Programmer's Manual*, Massachusetts Institute of Technology, 1962.

Ribbens, D., Programmation non numérique: LISP 1.5, *Monographie d'Informatique, AFCET*, Dunod, Paris, 1969.

Sandewall, E., 'Programming in an interactive environment: the LISP experience', *Computing Surveys*, Vol. 10, No. 1, March 1978.

Steele, G. L. and Sussman, G. J., *The Revised Report on SCHEME, a Dialect of LISP*, Massachusetts Institute of Technology, Artificial Intelligence Laboratory, Memo No. 452, Jan. 1978.

Tarvydas, P., 'A Potpourri of Utility Functions for LISP', *Dr Dobb's Journal of Computer Calisthenics and Orthodontia*, No. 38, Box E, Menlo Park, CA 94025, pp. 19-23.

Teitelman, W., 'CLISP: Conversational LISP', *IEEE Trans. on Computers*, Vol. C-25, No. 4, April 1976, pp. 354-357. [DWIM]

Wertz, H., 'Un système de compréhension de programmes incorrects', *3ème Colloque sur la Programmation, Paris* (Ed.: B. Robinet), pp. 31-49. [PHENARETE]

Winston, P. H. and Horn, B. K., *LISP*, Addison-Wesley, 1981.

15 Index of Quoted Functions